CH00780410

PROPHETS IN THE WILDERNESS

Prophets
in the Wilderness

THE WESLEYAN MISSION
TO NEW ZEALAND 1819-27

J. M. R. Owens

Auckland University Press : *Oxford University Press*

ISBN 0 19 647895 2

© J. M. R. Owens 1974

Printed in New Zealand
by Wright & Carman Ltd, Trentham

FOR DIANA

PREFACE

This book has been written over a period of years as one of a number of activities; and as the years have grown, so also the list of institutions and people whose help with the book and in other ways I gratefully acknowledge. The University of Auckland began and ended the process. It first brought me from England to be adult education tutor in Northland and thus placed me in a position, not unlike that of a missionary, in a region including the area covered by this book. It has finished the process by undertaking the full burden of publication. Victoria University of Wellington employed me when Mrs Mary Boyd of its History Department first suggested this topic to me and it was to Victoria that I submitted a Ph.D. thesis on the wider topic, 'The Wesleyan Mission to New Zealand, 1819-40.' Massey University, with which I became associated on the demise of Palmerston North University College (an off-shoot of Victoria), has provided or arranged all the support for my research: two periods of overseas study leave, a research grant from the funds of the University Grants Committee, support for travel, and the necessary resources and time for writing. The two periods of overseas leave enabled me to be associated with two other universities: the Institute of Historical Research of London University; and the Department of Pacific History at the Australian National University, which granted me a visiting fellowship to undertake projects which included the writing of this book. The Department of Pacific History, the unique creation of the late Professor J. W. Davidson, offered conditions for creative work that I have only elsewhere encountered as an undergraduate at Oxford: a privileged world in which, when you wished, you could count on being left alone, and

7

when you sought help, it overflowed. To all these universities my debt is obvious.

It is more difficult to acknowledge my debts to librarians and archivists and the institutions they serve, for their help has been so continuous and extensive it is now impossible to express individual appreciation. My continued acknowledgement of sources must be the memorial to their unfailing helpfulness. Since this is a book about Wesleyans, the friendly co-operation I have always received from present-day Methodists must be particularly acknowledged. The Methodist Missionary Society in London offered me daily hospitality and ready access to their holdings over a period of a year and the same unreserved assistance was offered by the Methodist Archives and Research Centre in London, the Methodist Connexional Office in Christchurch, and by Trinity Theological College in Auckland (which is shortly to be incorporated in the United College of St John the Evangelist). At many points my task was rendered easier by the activities of the Wesley Historical Society (New Zealand Branch) and its indefatigable secretary, the Rev. L. R. M. Gilmore.

Many individuals have helped me. Professors F. L. W. Wood, W. H. Oliver, Angus Ross, and J. W. Davidson have mainly helped by support and encouragement. The process of revising relevant chapters of my earlier thesis has been greatly assisted by comments and suggestions from Mrs Mary Boyd, Mrs Judith Binney, Dr Niel Gunson, and Mr Ormond Wilson. The detailed help received from Mrs Ruth Ross, whose knowledge of early Northland history is unrivalled, has earned particular gratitude. I am grateful also to Mr R. D. McEldowney of Auckland University Press for discovering slips which over-familiarity with the text had allowed me to miss. A different kind of help, no less essential, has come from Miss Heather Read, Secretary of the Massey History Department, who for years has turned my manuscripts into proper shape with cheerful skill. My wife, to whom this book is dedicated, has been involved in every way with its writing, which would have been impossible without her.

CONTENTS

LIST OF ILLUSTRATIONS

Portraits and drawings reproduced by permission of the owners, as indicated above.

10

PART ONE

I: ORIGINS

After all the negotiations and the pleading, the cajoling, after the touring and the making of speeches, after a successful hunt for a wife, the Reverend Samuel Leigh was off; not, this time, on a mission to Australia but, more excitingly, to 'the rude savages of New Zealand'. It was 17 January 1821; and at a Public Ordination Service in the New Chapel, City Road, London he and a Mr Morgan, who was to 'penetrate the dense negro population of the Gambia' received their instructions from the Committee of the Wesleyan Methodist Missionary Society.[1]

They were, said the instructions, going beyond the bounds of the British Empire, carrying their lives in their hands, much as did the first preachers of the Gospel. They were to set up schools, where the teaching of children was to be 'the first instrument for undermining the prejudices and superstitions of the heathen'. In giving instruction they should 'rather propose and enforce with meekness the glorious truths of the gospel, than dispute with their superstitious, and absurd opinions'; and as they were appointed to assist the natives in acquiring the knowledge of agriculture and some of the useful arts, they were themselves to cultivate, at least in the early stages of their mission, habits of labour and industry, but were to 'beware of the secular spirit'.

Leigh was to have 'a considerable quantity of hardware, implements of agriculture etc' to barter for food and timber; but he was not to engage in trade or acquire property. He was to take no part in civil affairs, but he could give advice beneficial to all parties when desired; he was to remonstrate against cruelty and to soften 'the barbarism of their manners'. The rules in the general Methodist instructions on the administration of baptism and on discipline in general were recommended to them for guidance. 'Our aim is not merely to civilize but to convert; and in every instance careful instruction in the Christian faith and evidence of a true turning of the heart unto the Lord is to be required before that sacred ordinance be administered.'

Both in New Zealand and on the banks of the Gambia, the missionary families were to live together in the mission house. The 'careful cultivation of the kindest brotherly affection' was solemnly enjoined. 'In honour prefer one another. Remember your great work: your brief and uncertain life; your solemn account. Live in peace, and the God of love and peace will be with you.'

Leigh's additional instructions recommended him to buy not more than 500 acres of land at a fair remuneration to the natives, for the use of the mission in New Zealand. He was to erect as soon as possible, premises for a school, a room for public worship, and three suites of apartments, one for each family, all under the same roof. There would be a common room in which meals would be taken together and family worship regularly performed. Each family would have for its separate use one sitting room and one sleeping room for the present. All articles for barter would be common stock; a secretary would enter in a book all articles of barter; no articles were to be used except by consent of two of the brethren when there were three of them; thereafter two-thirds of the whole. Copies of accounts of receipts and expenditures should be sent home in June and December of each year.

Each of the brethren should, by rotation, week by week, barter with the natives; each wife also, in weekly rotation, should take charge of the cooking when her husband bartered for food. Each missionary should have a fowling piece; but there should be no barter in muskets or war-like weapons.

Goods to the value of £50 a year were allowed for the support of schools; each married missionary would be allowed £50 a year, together with £12 a year for each child as quarterage. The society would send out as many suits of clothes as the missionary might order, this to be charged to

his account, the surplus paid in goods or cash as he might
direct. A sum not exceeding £40 a year would be allowed for
a supply of salt, butter, tea, coffee, sugar, soap, etc. from
New South Wales; £100 was allowed for the purchase of
cattle and other articles of subsistence from Botany Bay, if
necessary, together with £80 for furniture for the mission
house. Finally, that they might introduce a knowledge of
agriculture and useful arts among the natives, they were to
bring into cultivation as much of the land, which they would
purchase for mission use, as would supply them with 'the
necessaries of life'.

Thus it was all planned, with a suitable sense of occasion
and a proper regard to the loyalties of countless thousands
in chapels throughout the land. Yet there was nothing inevitable about New Zealand missions. They seemed logical enough
once launched; once European settlement began they seemed
only an early phase of a rational policy of British expansion.
But the Church Missionary Society had begun its mission in
1814 because of the constant badgering of Samuel Marsden;
now it was Samuel Leigh who had conjured the Wesleyan
mission into existence. There are grand sociological reasons
why each missionary body had thousands of supporters, willing
to be swayed; but if it be asked why the two New Zealand
missions began, in each case there is a prophet Samuel,
moving on levels part visionary, part mundane, at once altru-
istic and self-seeking, in both such a medley of motives nobody
should now be sure what moved them. Marsden and Leigh,
close friends for many years and alike in many ways, were
great planners of missionary projects and unexcelled in the
arts of public propaganda.

Leigh was the first Methodist missionary to Australia. A
present-day Methodist has called him 'an intense, single-
minded missionary, something of an introvert, almost a fanatic
by modern standards'.[2] On his first voyage to Australia, in
1815, if his own account is to be believed, his influence on
passengers and crew was hypnotic. The first attempt at card
playing dissolved when Leigh passed by, saying: 'Good night,
ladies and gentlemen. I pray God to save us this night from
destruction. On the Sabbath, mariners and passengers sat

about, reading the books and the tracts he had given out; the Captain went four months without an oath.[3]

His reception in Port Jackson in August 1815 was less gratifying: where, asked his host, was his furniture for a house? 'The Committee understood you,' said Leigh, 'to apply for furniture for a *horse*, and I have brought an excellent second-hand military saddle, bridle, and all other requisites'.[4] Yet it seems that, nothing daunted, he set about his task with vigour, winning the support not only of Marsden but also of Governor Macquarie, who was at first hostile. Within a few years he had established the first Methodist circuit with fourteen preaching places, which involved him in travelling 150 miles every three weeks. Under his impetus many chapels were built, the first at Castlereagh, another at Windsor on land given by Marsden; others in Macquarie Street and Princes Street.[5]

In May 1818, Leigh was joined by a young Cornish Methodist, in later life to be General Superintendent of the New Zealand mission, Walter Lawry. He also practised his calling on the voyage. One version has it that convicts, soldiers, and crew 'heard the word with gladness', and that the Captain's clerk trained a choir of singers.[6] Another has it that the loaded ship's gun was hidden behind the preacher; and soldiers with fixed bayonets stood each side of him. The Captain attributed convict good behaviour to a judicious mixture: boatswain's 'cat' before, preaching after. 'These men', wrote Lawry, 'need plain dealing, and they get it too. I enumerate their sins and crimes, not failing to appoint their inevitable doom (without repentance) among the deepest damned in the shades of hell.'[7]

Lawry's arrival was something of a crisis for Leigh who, with all his qualities as a pioneer, was now demonstrating limitations. The standard history of Methodist missions questions whether he knew how to husband his strength and whether his judgement, patience, and administrative skill equalled his powers of initiative.[8] He was now to show another defect, a tendency to quarrel with colleagues.

Lawry at first called Leigh everything he could wish; one who had been alone like a sparrow on the house-top, who had endured opposition, who had wandered in the forests without food, 'having no shelter by day, nor bed by night'.[9] Nonetheless, his first impression was that the Methodist interest was 'very low',[10] and by 1821, having clashed with Leigh on many points, his judgement of Leigh was harsh in the extreme. Out of this conflict grew Leigh's desire to carve a new area for himself in New Zealand.

In a number of ways, Lawry overshadowed Leigh. In Methodist writings he is summed up as 'country-bred, robust and cheerfully extrovert';[11] a man of 'vigour and attractive talent'.[12] He was the better preacher; Leigh's preaching, he said, was far below the mediocrity of local exhorters in Cornwall.[13] He was also more attractive to the ladies. According to Lawry, Leigh had made advances to Mary Hassall, daughter of a substantial landowner and merchant, who had been one of the London Missionary Society's party sent to evangelize Tahiti in 1796.[14] This, and not overwork, according to Lawry, was why Leigh's health had declined: 'having paid his addresses to a young lady and met a prompt repulse from her, the spring of his mind was observed to relax its force, and he never afterwards appeared to rejoice'.[15] No such repulse met Lawry; in January 1819 he proposed to the wealthy Miss Hassall; in November he was married.

The nature of Lawry's opposition is evident from the phrases he used in writing the Committee in London about Leigh, 'this weak and envious man'. He wrote of the vacancy of Leigh's mind, shown in stating a fact one day and the opposite the next; the 'sulky, magisterial, frowning manner in which he was accustomed to carry himself to me'; his 'idleness, jealousy, ignorance, selfishness and dishonourableness'. Many of their best members, Lawry thought, believed that Leigh had done little, if anything, towards the establishment of Methodism in the country. The toils and journeyings he had reported, were all suspect; 'and as to many of his other kinds of sufferings, such as no beds, no food etc, I believe, if ever a solitary instance of the kind occurred, it was when he was going across the country (not to preach) in search after a fair object'.[16]

In addition to rivalry in the pulpit, and in the pursuit of

fair (and wealthy) objects, there were also policy conflicts. Since coming to New South Wales, Leigh had followed the earlier Methodist practice of co-operation with the Anglican Church; he would not preach at times conflicting with their services, nor would he administer the sacrament where the clergy officiated. This policy followed Leigh's inclinations and his instructions on being sent out; it was reinforced by the spirit of friendly co-operation he and Marsden developed. But this approach was not likely to continue. It had prevailed in England during Wesley's lifetime; but following the 'Plan of Pacification' adopted by the Methodist Conference after his death, such co-operation was abandoned. Lawry and the others who followed him wished to follow the practice which had developed in England. Had there been no other issues, these conflicting views would have separated Leigh from his colleagues.[17]

So Leigh became ill; Lawry's view that it all arose from the state of his mind was to be echoed by others when Leigh suffered further illnesses later in his career. At this point, partly to recruit Leigh's health, Marsden offered him a trip to New Zealand to report on the state of the Church Mission in the Bay of Islands and Leigh accepted. He arrived at the Bay of Islands on 5 May 1819 on the *Active,* and stayed, apparently, until 17 June.[18]

Only fleeting glimpses are available of Leigh on this crucial visit. From William Hall's journal it appears that in company with John King he visited Hongi's settlement at Kerikeri, returning two days later; and that in company with Kendall he visited Whangaroa, which was to be the site of the first Wesleyan mission, and spent a night there.[19]

John King's journal refers to Leigh planting acorns in King's garden and reading sermons while Kendall prayed in Maori.[20] Strachan's life of Leigh, apparently drawing on Leigh's own reports, pictures him as a successful mediator in the conflicts between the CMS settlers; urging them to spend more time visiting the Maoris and to hold daily meetings for prayer and Bible reading and, in Methodist fashion, to form the surrounding villages into a circuit for regular visits. He may well have had a short-term influence; certainly he was well liked and corresponded with the settlers afterwards.[21]

Also in Strachan are references to tattooed human heads for sale; and to Leigh observing a naked 'pickanniny' in a 'Queen's' hut and wrapping it in a handkerchief to save its life (as he thought), only to lose the handkerchief for his pains.[22] John King also recorded his giving an axe for the body of a little boy, slain for stealing sweet potatoes from a Chief's *tapu* house and cut up for a cannibal feast. The remains were brought down to the settlement and buried 'in a piece meal way'; and when later they were half dug up and Leigh filled in the grave again, he was accused by the Maoris of working on the sabbath.[23]

He was, apparently, little recovered on his return to New South Wales, and, apparently, his return to England was on medical advice. At the mission house in Hatton Garden, London, he was interviewed by the secretaries, three of the great names of early nineteenth-century Methodism: the Rev. Jabez Bunting, so dominant a figure in Methodism he was to be nicknamed its Pope, the Rev. Joseph Taylor, and the Rev. Richard Watson. Leigh's plea for a mission to New Zealand and Tonga was met with the remark of Taylor that with a debt of £10,000 the Society could neither enlarge old nor undertake new missions.

But, as Strachan tells it, Leigh was obsessed with his plan, day and night; and finally he thought of a way. If the money was not available, he would go to the manufacturing districts and appeal for goods to establish a mission among the 'savage cannibals' of New Zealand. The scheme was referred to the Methodist conference at Liverpool and passed; Leigh was appointed missionary to New Zealand and toured the provinces appealing for goods; and in they poured. From an appropriately named Mr Holy, a hundred dozens of forks and knives; from Newton and Chambers of Thorncliffe, grates, pots, kettles, and 'sundries'; from one obviously fortunate lady, a hundred wedding rings; in Manchester, prints, calicoes, clothes, and 'curiosities', some over a hundred years old; in Birmingham, articles in copper, iron, and brass, saws of all kinds, axes, pins, buttons, and fish hooks; in Liverpool, clothes; and from a Captain Irving of Bristol a large tent.[24]

This motley collection was duly packed in old casks that had formerly contained wine, beer, and porter and sent on to New South Wales. Strachan asserted that it was 'received as a sacred deposit' and that it 'almost entirely supported the mission for five years'.[25] From incidental references the story appears more complicated; some was unusable, some damaged in transit, some rusted unused, some perhaps was sold, and much was used in New Zealand. The official history of the missionary society refers to 'disquieting criticism' of this mode of floating missions and admits candidly that it was impossible to trace the disposal of the several articles or to present an audited balance sheet of the transaction.[26] The mission society in fact spent £3,857 on the New Zealand mission in the five years 1820-24; whether all or any of this was raised by selling the goods donated, in either England or New South Wales, is not clear.[27] But as far as Leigh was concerned, doubtless the important point was that the objections had been overcome and the mission launched; and from the society's viewpoint, Leigh's appeal was probably useful in dramatizing its financial difficulties.

Leigh's attempt to arouse interest in New Zealand was greatly aided by the arrival of the two chiefs Hongi and Waikato, who reached England in July 1820 in company with Thomas Kendall of the CMS. For a while the two chiefs attracted great attention. They were received in audience with King George IV, as well as meeting a liberal assortment of dukes, earls, and bishops; and they visited the Tower, the British Museum, and a menagerie in the Strand.[28] In company with Kendall they also visited Professor Samuel Lee at Cambridge, to help in the production of a grammar and vocabulary of the New Zealand language.[29]

But the visit had not been with the approval of the CMS, which feared that what Hongi learnt of British civilization would not assist their own cause. In this they were correct. Hongi's recollections of the CMS were not happy;[30] by contrast he seemed favourably impressed with the Wesleyans, saying to Kendall, 'Mr Leigh got many friends, you got none'.[31]

When Hongi was received by the WMS he was presented

with a box of carpenter's tools and clothes for his wife. According to Strachan, he stayed for a while with Leigh, sleeping on the floor and thus obliging his host to follow suit; and in the same book is an anecdote, revealing not only the strain of this unaccustomed environment to Hongi, but also the insensitivity of his hosts. He was the guest of honour at the house of 'a highly respectable gentleman' and suddenly noticed some women apparently commenting on his tattooed face, with pitying smiles. In a state of excitement he threw himself across three chairs, covering his face with his hands and remaining in that posture until the company retired.[32]

In December 1820, Hongi, Waikato, and Kendall left England.[33] Leigh, after his public ordination service in January 1821, finally set sail in the *Brixton* on 28 April 1821 with 'a suitable assortment of goods' and in company with two other missionaries, William Horton, bound for Hobart Town, and William Walker, who was to devote himself to the 'Black Natives' of Australia.[34] Leigh by now was a married man; 'experience and observation', wrote Strachan in a somewhat enigmatic phrase, had long convinced him no single man should be appointed to labour amongst 'a barbarous people'. So, in 'the hope of promoting his own comfort, and extending his usefulness among the natives of New Zealand, he went down into Staffordshire and married a lady of the name of Clewes'.[35] They reached Sydney in September 1821.[36] Leigh was now known as 'General Superintendent of Missions to New Zealand and the Friendly Islands'.[37]

Back in England, two other men were preparing to join Leigh: William White and Nathaniel Turner. Little evidence has survived of White's early career. He was born in Durham, apparently in 1792, and his mother was Mrs Hannah White, of Ingleton, near Staindrop, Durham.[38] He was a carpenter by trade.[39] Nathaniel Turner, born at Wybunbury, Cheshire, in 1793, was one of a family of eight children. His father had a small farm, and the children were orphaned when Turner was nine years old. In adolescence he underwent a conversion experience, became a Methodist local preacher and then in 1819 a home missionary, working among the villages of Cheshire where, according to his own account, he received much opposition from squire and parson.[40] After hearing that he had been accepted for the New Zealand mission, Turner, like Leigh, went to Staffordshire for a wife and on 10 January 1822 married Ann, daughter of Mr John Sargent of Ipstones, Etruria. Mr Sargent is said to have opposed the idea of his daughter going to cannibal New Zealand but finally consented; and when the couple left for London, in the depths of winter with snow falling, more than a thousand friends are said to have gathered to farewell them.[41]

On 22 January 1822, the Leighs arrived in the Bay of Islands, in the *Active,* and took up residence in a barn at the CMS station at Rangihoua.[42] In London on 23 January, Turner and White were ordained at the Wesleyan Chapel, Greenwich, and the three Missionary Society secretaries, Bunting, Watson, and Taylor, participated in the service. According to Turner's later recollection there was some disapproval of the fact that White, who was now thirty, was going out unmarried; he had, in Joseph Taylor's phrase, 'fooled away his opportunities'.[43] For Mrs Turner, this increased the possibility, soon to be realized, of being the only missionary wife on the station.

They sailed for Van Diemen's Land and New South Wales on 15 February. There were twenty other cabin passengers, thoughtless ungodly men as Turner recollected them, some 'shamefully profane'. Yet he recorded also that much of the trouble with them was caused by the 'uneven temper and carriage' of William White. The missionaries appear to have kept apart, holding prayer meetings alternately in each other's cabins but proving their utility by successfully praying for a change of wind in the Bay of Biscay: 'Verily there is a god that heareth prayer.'[44] On 19 June they reached Hobart, where they were welcomed by the resident Methodist minister, William Horton and his wife.

Here Turner remained until the end of April the following year. He appears to have been put off proceeding to New Zealand partly by news of warfare following Hongi's return, and partly by concern over his wife's health. A daughter was born to them on 3 March 1823. In the meantime, Turner occupied himself among convicts and settlers. White, after a while, made his way to Sydney. On 20 January 1823, George Erskine, who had succeeded Leigh as General Superintendent for New South Wales and Van Diemen's Land[45] referred to White's arrival: 'a promising Missionary, diligent and fervent'.[46] Later the same month White also wrote from Sydney, apologizing for not sending extracts from his journal because his mind had been so 'distressed and dispirited by things which have transpired among the Brethren, the gloomy aspect which our affairs in this part of the world at present wear'.[47]

At the same time, three other men were being drawn into the mission. Leigh had at first said that no 'artificers' should accompany the missionaries in the South Sea Missions; but experience changed his views and by July 1822 he had written to the Sydney committee requesting two mechanics; and one of the New South Wales ministers was writing home expressing doubt: 'mechanics in general are very scarce, and nobody appears willing to venture on such a speculation'.[48] But Leigh was joined in the Bay of Islands by two men—Luke Wade, a sailor who was to serve the mission for many years as a general handy man and servant, and James Stack, who had arrived unannounced after listening to one of Leigh's addresses in New South Wales. He was a man of small stature and of little use in the pioneering toil of Wesleydale; but his intelligence and education enabled him to be the first among them to make progress in the Maori language and he proved invaluable as an interpreter, preacher, teacher, doctor, and accountant. Stack had a varied background. He was born on 1 September 1801 at Portsmouth. His family were of Irish Catholic descent, but his father having changed his religion, Stack was baptized into the Church of England. From the age of nine to fourteen he served in the Navy. The family then removed to Ireland for three and a half years, where he veered between Catholic and Methodist influences; then he and a brother emigrated to New South Wales where after acting as a storekeeper at a farm of John Macarthur he went to sea on H.M. Sloop *Bathurst* (Captain P. King) which was surveying the passage through Torres Straits, Dampier's Archipelago, and various parts of the coast of New Holland. It was, wrote Stack later, very hazardous navigation;

but worse, he was the butt of ridicule for not 'conforming to the sinful taste of my corrupt and depraved equals', and a 'gay young officer' used to pass his 'wicked jokes' about Stack reading the scriptures. Back in Sydney he attended services of the Church of England and of the Methodists. A Methodist merchant arranged a free passage to New Zealand for him and he arrived there in February 1823, where, after some demur, Leigh received him on trial as an assistant missionary.[49]

Turner, for his part, had recruited John Hobbs, a Kentish local preacher who had arrived in Van Diemen's Land early in 1823. Born on 22 February at St Peter's, Isle of Thanet, Hobbs was of old Puritan stock. His father, Richard Hobbs, a coachbuilder, had been admitted into the Methodist Society by John Wesley and was one of his local preachers. Brought up with pious care by his father, Hobbs was often 'greatly alarmed by the thunders of the divine law' and affected by 'Representations of a Saviour's dying love'. At sixteen he underwent a conversion experience and for four months 'seldom experienced a gleam of Hope; but lived in a fearful looking for of Judgement, and fiery indignation'. Finally one evening, 'ruminating on my miserable condition, I felt resolved if I must perish, it should be at the foot of my dying Saviour's cross'. By close attention to the Scriptures he decided it was not God's will 'to contend forever; neither to be always wroth, lest the spirit should fail before him. . . . And though I received no instantaneous Gusts of divine Love, yet my Faith and Love increased, until I was enabled to embrace Christ as my Saviour, and steadfastly believe I had redemption in His Blood, the forgiveness of all my sins'.[50]

Hobbs left England on 4 July 1822[51] for Van Diemen's Land, 'that Sink of Iniquity and Pollution', which he reached on 23 November.[52] He was accompanying his friend Pullen, a local preacher in the Margate circuit, who, said Hobbs, was emigrating 'for the Kingdom of Heaven's sake',[53] and years later it was claimed that Hobbs had gone 'to try and ameliorate the spiritual condition of the degraded convict population'.[54] Towards the end of April 1823, Turner sailed for Sydney with his wife and infant daughter and on 30 June,

at a meeting there of the committee overseeing the South Sea
missions, he reported that Hobbs had offered his services for
the New Zealand mission, that he was 'well qualified to be
useful in New Zealand, being by trade a Carpenter and Joiner
and Blacksmith and being a man of amiable disposition, of
good talents and genuine piety'.[55] The committee resolved
that as Leigh had asked for a mechanic, he should be engaged;
and on 10 July, Hobbs having arrived, he was engaged as a
mechanic for two years at £30 a year; he was to repay a
debt of £40 he owed, by £20 a year; was to be supplied with
food and board; and if 'the female friend, whom he has
named as his intended wife' arrived in Sydney, she was to be
lodged, supported, and forwarded to New Zealand. If married,
his salary was to be £50 a year. His outfit was to consist of
two suits of working clothes, six shirts, four pairs of shoes,
four silk handkerchiefs, six pairs of stockings, and a Flushing
coat.[56]

While these developments were taking place, Leigh and his
wife, and later Wade and Stack, had been living with William
Hall for sixteen months, eating at one table as one family,
as Hall put it.[57] In this period Leigh can virtually be considered a member of the CMS mission and as such became
involved in the disputes revolving around Thomas Kendall.[58]
In this, Leigh took the side of the Rev. John Butler, with
whom he was on terms of personal friendship.[59]

Various reasons were given why Leigh did not move
off to begin his own separate mission. The main one was the
warfare following Hongi's return from England, which prevented Leigh from going to Mercury Bay.[60] As Leigh reported
it, in Hongi's absence a relative had been slain by friends at
Mercury Bay and the River Thames. Hongi declared war on
them, collected three thousand men, and on his return claimed
to have slain a thousand men and to have roasted and eaten
three hundred before leaving the battlefield. He killed the
chief, Hinaki, whom he had met in New South Wales, cut off
his head, poured the blood into his hands and drank it.[61]
Kendall, however, asserted it would have been as safe for
Leigh to settle elsewhere as it had been for Kendall to settle
in the Bay of Islands seven years earlier——an assertion which

Leigh said was 'as full of hypocrisy as his heart is of fornication'.[62]

Another of Leigh's reasons was that he was awaiting White's arrival, having been advised by the CMS it was imprudent to start on his own. He also claimed that he was learning to speak Maori. He would gather his listeners into a circle to 'repeat a letter, and to spell a word, such as ma-du, when all the heathens with pleasure repeated after me both letters and words for half an hour together. On my retiring from them they have requested me to *crack hear*, that is to say more'.[63] According to Strachan, Leigh and his wife also wrote prayers and hymns in English and with the assistance of the CMS translated them into Maori for use in open-air services.[64]

It has frequently been claimed that Leigh in this period became something of a Maori linguist.[65] This was not the view of his fellow missionaries. Lawry thought that in a fortnight he and his wife had learnt more Maori than Leigh had in six months; and Turner on arrival reported that after eighteen months in the country, with little else to do but learn the language, Leigh was 'not able to string ten sentences together or speak to the natives on the commonest subjects'.[66] Although Leigh was perhaps the most glaring example of a poor linguist, none of the early members of the mission had received any prior training in languages and this was to be a major stumbling block.

Leigh showed some enlightenment in his view that 'until we know thier ways thier superstitious system we shall not be able to reason with them on the subjects error or be able to shew unto them the more excellent way and the True God in whom we believe'. He described the wreck of the American vessel *Cossack* (Captain Dix) on the River Gambier (Hokianga) as being caused, in the Maori view, by 'the anger of their God of the wind and the sea' residing in two large rocks at the entrance to the harbour, which members of the crew had trespassed upon.[67] But in this he appears merely to have been reporting what he learnt from his CMS colleagues; and although he wrote about *tapu*, burial customs, the spirit world, cannibalism, Maori dislike of swearing, and willingness to observe the Sabbath, he showed no originality or perceptiveness in what he wrote. Indeed, many of the anecdotes he sent home show strong resemblance to stock missionary accounts he must have read.

In July 1822, Leigh and the CMS were visited by Walter Lawry and his wife, bound for Tonga in the ship *St Michael* (Captain Beveridge). The two had continued to clash after Leigh's return from Sydney, when, to Lawry's surprise, Leigh had brought news that Lawry was also appointed to New Zealand.[68] Lawry had strongly opposed this. Later, he was appointed to Tonga. Finding it difficult to obtain a vessel, Lawry, who since his marriage was a man of substance, bought the *St Michael*, and when he sailed still had a third share in it. Although Lawry was criticized for having a financial interest in what was ostensibly a missionary expedition, there was probably no other way he could have made the trip.[69]

Lawry felt that Leigh was manoeuvring him out of New South Wales. He did not pull any punches in his letters to the London committee; in addition to his strictures on Leigh's earlier career, already quoted, he also charged that before his return to Britain Leigh had made a regular contract of marriage to another young lady, whose friends would not allow her to marry Leigh in view of his poor health. Nonetheless, she expected Leigh to marry her on his return from Britain and in the meantime rejected two suitors. When the news came that a Mrs Leigh was also arriving, she hoped this might be his mother; and continued to cherish 'her passions and expectations concerning him unto the very last'. Her hopes finally dashed, she kept to her room for days. 'I have written this letter', said Lawry in a postscript, 'because I had been apprized that Mr L. had lowered me in the eyes of my brethren and because I believe that Mr L. is a *useless, idle person.* May the Almighty bring good out of evil—and save our souls from hell.'[70]

All of this was in the background when on 12 July 1822 the Lawrys and Captain Beveridge and his wife dined ashore with the Halls and the Leighs. Afterwards they called the ship's company on the quarter deck, sang a hymn, gave the sailors 'a caution relative to the native women, who were

crowded on the deck', and then kneeled and gave God
thanks for a safe passage—'a time of uncommon feeling and
great devotion'.[71] There was much to learn of the Bay of
Islands: Mr Kendall's 'sinful and unnatural intercourse with
a native girl', his haranguing the natives to murder the missionaries and his attempts to burn Hall's house; the poor girl,
formerly in the keeping of 'poor unfortunate Samuel Butler',
now a common strumpet; and Mr Cowell, of whom Leigh and
Hall gave a very indifferent account.[72]

On the 15th, a rainy day with the ladies ashore, Lawry
and Captain Beveridge amused themselves drinking with 'Old
Kerra Kerra', who would drink a health, saying, 'How do
do sir', and, pouring in his glass say, 'Thank e sir'. Lawry
observed that many Maoris had a great deal of information
about European habits and manners, but seemed perfectly
wedded to their own ways. 'They say Karakia (prayer) is very
well; but Mr Marsden moe moe (sleep) while Mr Cowper
Karakia in Sydney Church.'[73] On the other days there were
services, or social visits such as one to the Rev. John Butler
at Kerikeri.

Lawry and his party finally left on 28 July and he recorded
that he and Leigh had forgotten their former misunderstanding and did all they could to 'lighten each other's burden in
our share of woe'.[74] Nonetheless he saw much to criticize.
New Zealand, he thought, was 'a very dismal place'. The
natives had killed and eaten many people since their arrival,
in sight of the ship. He had travelled or sailed over two
hundred miles but not seen any good land; timber was scarce.
The missionaries reckoned there were not more than ten
thousand people in the island. The people appeared little
benefited by the CMS mission, nor were they likely to be
benefited by 'men merely sent to teach them to saw timber
and other mechanical arts. Messrs King and Hall told me
that some of the men whom they had instructed for many
years were the most blood thirsty and savage. It is the word
of God, and not axes and saws, that must convert the heathen
world'. He was not in despair of the New Zealanders' conversion, but thought they were some of the most unlikely
people in the world. As for Leigh, living very comfortably

with a CMS mechanic, he did not know how to act: he thought of going to the North Cape.[75]

It was not until 16 November that Leigh wrote home about Lawry. By this time there was little evidence of reconciliation. Lawry had gone to Tonga, said Leigh, but had little intention of staying there. He had taken five men at the expense of the society and most of the articles from the stores in New South Wales belonging to the New Zealand mission. He was partner in the vessel and had gone on a trading voyage to the islands but at the expense of the missionary society. While in the Bay of Islands they bought articles from Maoris for gunpowder and had overcharged Leigh for bringing goods from New South Wales. 'The conduct of Mr Lawry in New Zealand has done more evil than I fear I shall ever do good.'[76]

During the period it is claimed Leigh made 'voyages of investigation . . . attended with constant danger; repeatedly his life was threatened'.[77] In fact, only two such expeditions are recorded. An undated visit to Whangaroa is described in Strachan; Leigh, it is claimed, hired 'a fisher's boat and five natives' and set off for Whangarei, ending up instead at Whangaroa (which, since they are in the opposite directions, suggests he had his limitations either as navigator or linguist). They spent a night with the Whangaroa Maoris, who could be heard quarrelling about the time for roasting and eating them next day; and after a conversation with the chief 'Tara', or George, about the massacre of the crew of the *Boyd,* Leigh prepared to leave. At this point he saw 'a numerous body of naked savages rushing upon him with spears, brandishing their clubs, assuming the most terrific attitudes and uttering the most discordant and unearthly yells'. Leigh took from his pocket a handful of fish hooks, kindly donated by Messrs Turner and Co., of Birmingham, threw them over their heads, and while the naked savages scrambled for their loot, the intrepid missionary made his escape.[78]

This account appears to be based on stories Leigh told in later life. It can be questioned on several grounds. There is no contemporary independent confirmation. Leigh is unlikely to have gone on such an expedition unaccompanied by other Europeans. He had visited Whangaroa in 1819, but in a ship's boat in company with Thomas Kendall and Charles Gordon of the CMS and there is no record of such adventures then.[79] The account appears a mixture of this visit and of the later expedition when the Whangaroa mission was established after a visit to Whangarei. In his account of the later expedition, Leigh makes no reference to an earlier visit, though he does refer to sending a portrait of George and an account of him about twelve months earlier.[80]

There is however independent confirmation of Leigh's visit to Oruru at the end of March 1823.[81] He was accompanied by the Rev. John Butler and five Maoris in Butler's boat. (From a reference in Leigh's journal to the Europeans, it is possible Stack and Wade also accompanied them, but they are not named.) Hongi had suggested Oruru because his sister lived there. They sailed north past the Cavalli Islands and Whangaroa to Doubtless Bay, where they went ashore and spent the night. Next day they proceeded twelve miles up the river to the village where Hongi's sister lived. Leigh gave her an axe and gave everyone fish hooks, in return for which they were given baskets of sweet potatoes. Their welcome was warm and Hongi's sister urged them to stay and start a mission—but, according to Butler, they stayed no more than half an hour because the tide was turning. They decided against Oruru as a missionary settlement, because it had no harbour for shipping, its river was not navigable even for a boat (although they had in fact gone up it in a boat), and the population appeared small.

Butler commented that it was a hazardous business going in an open boat on the stormy coast. Leigh also commented on this, claiming with some exaggeration they had travelled four hundred miles; and he referred also to God's preservation of them when they 'placed themselves, for Christ's sake, in the hands of the dark sons of the forest, many of whom never before saw the face of a white man . . .'[82] On the other hand, it was an expensive two-night trip, not only in the largesse distributed by Leigh but in the refreshments consumed: 'One piece of salt pork, seven pounds; one piece of bacon, seven pounds; three quarts of rice; one and a half pound of tea; three and a half pounds of sugar; six bottles of porter; two bottles of brandy; three hundred fish-hooks; twelve knives, four razors; six pairs of scissors; and two axes. To four natives who navigated the boat, one hundred and fifty fish-hooks.'[83]

It was an abortive trip, but all Leigh's months as a missionary had been abortive so far. But the men and the equipment and the stores were assembling and the project was about to begin, thanks to the inspiration, the drive, the vision, and the mean-spirited jealousies of Samuel Leigh.

II: EARLY DAYS AT WHANGAROA

On 16 May 1823 the irascible and tireless William White arrived in the Bay of Islands with stores for the mission, on the *St Michael* (Captain Beveridge);[1] despite a month's tedious passage he was in good health 'and by the help of God resolved to devote my future days to his glory and to the good of our fellow creatures'.[2] Within a month a separate mission had been started and he was slogging away at the hard physical toil needed to erect a mission station from nothing.

One of the first points noted by White was the warmth of his reception by the CMS: at Kerikeri, for example, they were 'received in the most cordial and affectionate manner by the Rev. John Butler and all the settlers, who seemed to vie with each other in expressing their pleasure at the arrival of more help in the great work of evangelizing the heathen'.[3] He was invited to preach at Kerikeri and at Rangihoua and at both places met members of the CMS with whom he was to be closely involved in future years: John King, William Hall, James Kemp, and James Shepherd.[4] In company with Butler's son Samuel, he visited Waimate, spending a night in a Maori village. He was almost as horrified by the Maori habit of eating lice as he was by tales of cannibalism; nor was it pleasant himself to acquire 'several head of livestock'; but he supposed custom would render it more tolerable.[5]

Preparations were going ahead for the proposed settlement at Whangarei. On 21 May, Butler handed over trees and garden seeds, together with a cow, a calf, and some goats.[6] The following day he received a letter from Leigh thanking him for all his past kindness and formally requesting his company on the forthcoming expedition.[7]

On 26 May the *St Michael* left Rangihoua. The party included Leigh and White (and presumably also Mrs Leigh and Stack and Wade) and from the CMS, Butler, Hall, and Mr and Mrs Shepherd. On their way to Whangarei they passed war canoes returning to the Bay of Islands and learnt that Hongi had destroyed four fortified places and had a musket ball through his helmet just above the head.[8] The same evening they reached Whangarei harbour and the next few days were spent in a ship's boat exploring the harbour and creeks, looking for a suitable mission site. But although they found several hundred acres of level fertile ground near to the river and plenty of fine timber, there were almost no people. Formerly populous villages had been plundered and burnt by war parties about twelve months earlier;[9] the warriors, reported Butler, had 'dragged their children about by the hair of their heads, and kicked them about on the ground like dogs'.[10] White was even more horrified to notice the putrefying leg of a slave, the rest of her body eaten, left in a tree, he assumed as a sacrifice. 'Oh! how horrible that the race of Adam should thus kill and eat each other.'[11]

On 2 June a committee meeting was held with Captain Beveridge in the chair. Five local chiefs had been invited aboard and had been most anxious that Leigh and his companions should settle there. But the committee decided instead to go north to Whangaroa.[12] In the afternoon White took his fowling piece ashore and shot several small birds. Perhaps it was a pretext to be alone and think. 'My mind', he wrote, 'is not so spiritual as it should be. Trifling and liberty overcome me . . . paralysing my soul in the exercising of spiritual things; I feel that pride is certainly gaining ground upon me I cannot bear anything like disrespect, as I ought or as I once could.'[13]

As they were leaving, the ship was stuck on a sandbank for six hours, floating off when the tide turned. There was much alarm, White wrote; many wept. Some saw it an omen from God they should not be leaving a people who had welcomed them and who had wept at the news they were leaving.[14] 'In this great deliverance', wrote Leigh, 'we have seen the good hand of our God. . . .'[15] On 5 June they reached Whangaroa.

In contrast to Whangarei, Whangaroa was heavily popu-
lated. There were two tribes living in the harbour. Near the
heads were Ngatipou, under Te Pere; further inland were
the Ngatiuru, led by the brothers Te Puhi, Te Aara, who
was also known as George, and Ngahuruhuru.[16] These two
tribes lived in a condition of latent hostility that was out-
wardly forgotten much of the time, but became evident
whenever opportunity encouraged it. According to a later
missionary report, there were two hundred Ngatiuru and six
to seven hundred Ngatipou.

The origins of these two tribal groups are not altogether
clear. S. Percy Smith said that Ngatiuru migrated to this
area about the year 1770-5, 'having been driven from Whanga-
mumu, South of the Bay of Islands and the southern shores
of the Bay itself, because their chief (Kuri) killed Marion du
Fresne, which led to a war with the Bay of Islands people'.[17]
Other writers have said that this tribe was Ngatipou.[18] Percy
Smith, however, wrote that Ngatipou 'formerly occupied the
whole of the country round Waimate and Ohaeawae, the
country known as Tai-a-mai. A tribe named Ngati-Miru and
another named Te Wahine-iti occupied at the same time as
Ngati-Pou, and was driven out or exterminated by Nga-
Puhi'.[19] However tenuous such background evidence may be,
it helps emphasize that the inter-tribal conflicts which were
to occur during the mission period had deep roots in the
pre-European period.

As a centre of missionary activity, Whangaroa was far less
influenced by European contact than the Bay of Islands.
Nonetheless, there had been contact, contrary to the frequent
assertion of missionary supporters that missionaries were the
pioneers of European contact in New Zealand; and the pre-
missionary contact was to have consequences which affected
mission influence.

Whangaroa had much to command it as a place for
shipping to visit. It had timber and water and a population
capable of developing resources of pigs and potatoes for trade.
It was also, as Cruise remarked, 'one of the finest harbours
in the world; the largest fleet might ride in it, nor is there a
wind from which it is not sheltered'.[20] But perhaps because

of their memories of Marion du Fresne's visit and associated violence—twenty-seven Europeans killed, but at least three hundred Maoris killed in return—the people of Whangaroa soon gained a reputation for treachery with European shipping. Whangaroa also lagged behind the Bay of Islands in European contacts because its entrance, though deep quite close to land on each side, was not more than half a mile wide and impossible to discover from any distance at sea.[21] Hence it does not appear to have been entered by a European vessel until 1807, when the *Star* (Captain Wilkinson) is recorded as being there.[22]

Either at this point,[23] or on its visit to New Zealand in 1809, the young chief George sailed with the *Star,* from which he is later recorded as having transferred to the ill-fated *Boyd.*[24] In 1808 the brig *Commerce* (Captain Ceroni), with the Bay of Islands chief Te Pahi on board, visited Whangaroa en route for Sydney.[25] There is some evidence that in the wake of this visit an epidemic occurred, killing many, including chief 'Kytoke'. It was said that Ceroni had dropped his watch, regarded as his *atua,* in the sea and this event was associated with the outbreak.[26] European disease and an existence ruled by the clock thus made their first rude onslaught on the people of Whangaroa.

In 1809 the *Boyd* visited Whangaroa and her crew and passengers, with the exception of a woman and two children, were killed. The reason usually given was that George was one of the crew and was flogged by the captain's orders, an intolerable affront to a *rangatira,* and hence the ship was lured to Whangaroa and *utu* exacted. This difference between the European and Maori attitude to flogging was to be an issue when the missionaries settled. However, William Williams later learnt another version which attributed the attack, not to the ill-treatment of George, but to the epidemic.[27] Hugh Carleton later stated that old Maoris were emphatic that the instigator of the massacre was not George but Pipikoitareke of Ngatiuru.[28] Pipikoitareke was blown up in an accident with gunpowder on the *Boyd* and George on his deathbed was to worry about exacting *utu,* all of which was to have its effect on the missionaries.

The ramifications of the *Boyd* affair were many. At the time it was widely believed that the Bay of Islands chief, Te Pahi, who was well known for his visits to Port Jackson and for his encouragement of Europeans, was involved; and a group of whalers attacked his island stronghold. It is equally possible he had no part in it and that Europeans with a poor ear for Maori confused his familiar name with Te Puhi and Te Pere, both of whom are more likely to have been involved. Other tribes, jealous of Te Pahi's leading position in European trade, or anxious to divert the blame, could have helped consolidate the mistake. George, many years later, for example, dictated a letter to the authorities in New South Wales attempting to involve all the surrounding tribes, including those at Kerikeri, Te Puna, and the Hokianga, in responsibility for the killing.[29]

The affair created or increased enmity between the people of the northern Bay of Islands and Whangaroa. It led to a decline of shipping visits which affected the supply of muskets to the Bay of Islands as well as Whangaroa; this meant that neighbouring tribes were always likely to avenge any future attacks on shipping as a threat to their own security. Marsden later recorded George telling him 'how he had been despised and insulted for cutting off the *Boyd* by the different tribes, and what trouble it had given him, as they would not be reconciled to him on that account'.[30] Ngatiuru, and particularly George, were left with a continual dread of a European punitive expedition; and European disease was attributed to the vengeance of the European god.[31]

There are not many records of European ships visiting Whangaroa after the *Boyd* affair. In December 1814, Marsden in company with Ruatara and Hongi visited Whangaroa and met with George and Te Puhi to make the peace between the two tribes. Leigh and Kendall came in 1819 and then in 1820, as a result of a visit by Marsden, the store ship H.M.S. *Dromedary* (Captain Richard Skinner) came to obtain kauri spars.[32] Dr Fairfowl, surgeon on the *Dromedary,* later said he believed no whalers had visited Whangaroa since the attack on the *Boyd* and the Maoris did not appear to have more than five muskets, three of them unserviceable.[33] The impact of the *Dromedary* visit was therefore considerable, particularly as it stayed from 22 June to 30 November, during which time Whangaroa was also visited by the schooner *Prince Regent* (Captain J. R. Kent), and the whaler *Saracen*.

The kauri spars were obtained with great labour which involved the building of a road for a mile and a half over undulating ground intersected with a swamp and a brook. The Ngatiuru chiefs were paid nearly a hundred axes: according to Cruise, George received them with a sneer, asking what he was to do with them?[34] Many items were exchanged during this period: ships' biscuits but also hatchets, axes, saws, spades, hoes, and iron tools—so much so that Dr Fairfowl noted they became over-stocked and indifferent to such items.[35] Though the *Dromedary* sought to avoid doing so, before leaving for Port Jackson they exchanged muskets and so also did the *Saracen*. The Maoris for their part traded hogs, potatoes, cabbage, turnips, peas, and fish. To clear ground for planting, fires were lit which got out of hand, so that Cruise reported the whole country 'in a blaze'.[36]

The Maoris also provided the sailors and soldiers with women, many of whom lived on the ship permanently. Some of the crew, such as a young midshipman, formed such strong affections they had to be brought back to the ship by force, and there was violence from Te Puhi when women from the Bay of Islands came on board the vessel.[37] 'Prostitution', reported Dr Fairfowl, 'is not reckoned a crime or a disgrace amongst the unmarried women, and the chiefs come and offer their sisters and daughters for prostitution and expect a present in return.'[38] Later, when the missionaries denounced polygamy as a sin, they were asked, why then did the pakehas of the *Dromedary* live with Maori women?[39]

It is clear that by the time the missionaries arrived, the people of Whangaroa had learnt the full economic advantages of having resident Europeans and had developed some skill in providing services and a keen sense of values in articles exchanged. Their women had a close knowledge of the ways of British men; and the guns of the *Dromedary* having been demonstrated, they were all aware of the military resources which could be brought against them if they offended their

visitors. They had also learnt enough to judge that missionaries were not speaking for all Europeans in some of the
claims they made. Whangaroa had not felt European influence
as fully as the Bay of Islands; but most of the usual points
of contact had been made.

These visitors also left descriptions of the Maoris which
can usefully be compared with later missionary accounts.
Captain Skinner began with the familiar European complaint
—'the natives' were unequal to the labour required: 'they
generally work tolerably well for a few days, but as soon as
the novelty of their occupation has subsided, and they have
got possession of a few trifling articles, we can get no further
exertions from them'.[40] Chiefs, he said, had not the least
authority over their tribes; it was difficult to distinguish them
from other Maoris as they all appeared to dress, live, and
work alike. However, when Cruise first visited Te Puhi,
George's elder brother 'and, of course, the greater chief' (a
distinction the missionaries took much longer to learn), he
found him seated at the door of his hut, dressed in new mats,
painted, and decorated with feathers.[41] Te Puhi's house,
recently built, was one of the largest they had seen.

The visitors formed a clear judgement of the three Ngatiuru
chiefs: 'Ehoodoo' (Ngahuruhuru), said Cruise, was 'a quiet,
industrious, and well-conducted man; but his two brothers
were, without exception, the most troublesome and the worst-
disposed chiefs we had met in New Zealand'.[42]

This was shown in the ever-present danger of treacherous
attack; also in many instances of animosity between the two
tribes in the harbour. Captain Skinner painted an almost
Hobbesian picture of them: 'they are extremely treacherous,
and suspicious, and no force of argument will convince them
of your intentions whenever they have a doubt, so much are
they accustomed to deception in their neighbours; hence,
promises have little or no weight with them; and I have in
no instance discovered the least spark of gratitude among
them, nor do they seem to possess such a feeling.'[43] Unlike
the Bay of Islanders they had not learnt to disguise their
cannibalism; and infanticide of female children was common.

He added that they were by no means as formidable a race

as he had been led to believe: a hundred armed soldiers might march from one end of New Zealand to another; nor would twenty armed men be attacked unless it could be done by surprise. Cruise commented that the firelocks the Maoris had been given were almost useless and badly maintained; stones were often used instead of bullets. To shoot a pigeon they would cautiously climb a tree and place the muzzle of the gun within a foot of the bird before pulling the trigger. Yet in inter-tribal fighting the mere possession of guns, however ineffective in practice, was a means of inspiring terror. *Pa* had generally been abandoned since the introduction of muskets, though Te Puhi's people lived at the foot of a *pa* which was 'on a circular hill, steep and difficult of ascent' in the middle of the valley of the river Kaeo; and pre-European weapons, such as *mere* and *patu patu* were being replaced by bayonets, axes, and tomahawks.[44]

Apart from the fact that missionaries did not comment on military capacity, these remarks were not notably different from those they were to make.

William White's first impression of Whangaroa seems to have been the magnificence of its scenery. They had anchored on the evening of Thursday 6 June between the heads of Whangaroa harbour, so near land they could hear Maoris talking on shore. Next morning at daybreak they found themselves quite landlocked and surrounded by canoe loads of Maoris. The tips of high mountains showed over a morning mist; when it cleared, 'the scenery which burst upon our view was the most Grand, Majestic, Romantic and pleasing that I had ever seen'. Nearby was a small but tremendously high island (doubtless Te Pere's island), on the side of which was 'a very large and populous village', and as far as the eye could see up the harbour were beautiful bays, villages, and abundance of land in cultivation.[45]

After breakfast, Leigh, Butler, Hall, and White set off by boat for George's place, further up the harbour. They passed the wreck of the *Boyd*, where they could see the logs of 'cedar' in her hold, and then went on to a fresh water river where they met George. When they landed, the chiefs George and

Te Puhi had ordered a feast of pork and potatoes; they were not only willing but anxious that the missionaries should settle among them. White noted it as a most suitable place to settle. There were great numbers of people, abundant timber and water, and good land. George came to the ship and entertained them with his 'shrewd and sensible answers to various questions', and here also they were joined by the third brother, Ngahuruhuru.

On Sunday they held service, both Leigh and Butler preaching.[46] During the following week they set up shelter by the side of the river on the *Dromedary's* landing place; on the opposite side was the spot where the Captain and crew of the *Boyd* had been killed and eaten.[47] Ground was cleared for the tent which was erected, a wharf was made for landing goods, and a road and a bridge improvised to the tent site. It was decided also that Butler and the ship's carpenter should erect a log house, thirty feet by fifteen and thatched with raupo. This involved going into the nearby bush and felling the timber required.

Most of the time it rained and in addition the tent leaked. Leigh, in order to escape what he called the 'heavy due' coming through the canvas, took to sleeping in a wine cask in which goods had been brought.[48] Already his health was beginning to suffer in the primitive conditions. Yet one evening when White went outside the tent, he was astonished to see that despite the dew and the cold, seven or eight Maoris could be seen sleeping peacefully close together in the open air. 'What is it that custom and habit can not do?' he commented. He himself thrived on privation: 'tho' I am day after day baithed in Presperation and sometimes up to the middle in Water and covered with mud and withal exposed to the night air very frequently, yet I do not catch cold, my health, appetite and spirits are as good as ever I knew them to be. Praise the Lord!'[49]

On 24 June, Butler left and the following day, William Hall.[50] The house was mostly built before Butler left; the frame up, the sides and ends logged, the fronts weatherboarded and one course of thatch on the roof.[51] When White wrote Butler a letter of thanks on 13 July, paying tribute to his work 'exposing yourself to all the wet and cold, and plodding in the dirt', he was able to say they had moved into the house, the Leighs living in the lower room and Mr and Mrs Shepherd in the west end upstairs. White had erected a chimney at the west end and on the 10th he wrote that the Leighs had left the tent and they all sat round a good fire. Leigh attempted family prayer that evening but was so affected he could not proceed.[52] When Turner arrived in August he described the house as humble and uncomfortable. By then it had four apartments, two above and two below; one of the ground-floor rooms was the store, where Luke Wade slept, and the other was the kitchen and parlour.[53]

At this point it is not easy to assess the work done by the various people in the missionary party. James Stack does not appear to have sent back any reports at this stage and it can be guessed that because of his physique he was given the the lighter duties. There are occasional references to Wade the ex-sailor handyman; and Shepherd of the CMS, despite a clash with White, appears to have been useful in pioneering and in preaching.[54] At about the beginning of August his wife gave birth to a son, the first child to be born there.[55] It is more difficult to assess the part played by Leigh and his wife, in comparison to White. Strachan's life of Leigh ignores White and greatly inflates Leigh's role and this has been followed in the standard detailed accounts of the mission. This emphasis was probably influenced by White's later reputation and by the anecdotes Leigh grew accustomed to telling in later life in England.[56] In the Strachan version, Leigh was an heroic peacemaker in the manner of Henry Williams of the CMS, and an industrious, resourceful pioneer, making bricks out of local clay, improvising lime out of burnt cockle shells, and building the chimney for the house.[57] The contemporary documents, however, show his colleagues, not Leigh, performing these tasks and there is ample evidence that his ill-health rendered any great exertion impossible. For example, on 20 July he wrote: 'It is nearly three months since I have been able to attend to any part of my duty as a missionary. Like unto a broken pitcher I have been laid quite on one side. . . . The nature of my disease is a general weakness, with cough, and pain in my chest, and throat, with great pain in my head, and dimness of sight. . . . My constitution appears to be so much shook that I fear I shall not be able to take an active part in the mission.'[58]

Luckily, reinforcements soon arrived. On 5 August a chief fired off a musket to salute some white men who had appeared in the distance and when White set off with some men to carry them across the river, to his great joy he met 'my dear Brother Turner accompanied by Mr Hobbs. . . .'[59] The *Brampton* had arrived in the Bay of Islands two days earlier with Marsden, Henry Williams with family and servants, William Fairburn and family, together with the two Wesleyans and Turner's wife and six-month old daughter and a young girl servant, Betsy.[60] While Marsden plunged into the intricate problems of his mission, Hobbs and Turner, wasting no time, had walked overland with two of Butler's Maoris to see their future home.

After a night, Turner returned to the Bay of Islands to see about bringing round the rest of the stores. Hobbs was already labouring hard; helping with the house, making a road into the wood, and hauling logs of kauri out to the river.[61] 'Mr Hobbs', wrote White, 'appears to be a true disciple of Jesus Christ and full of missionary zeal and we hope he will be very useful.'[62]

When the captain of the *Brampton* refused to go round to Whangaroa, Turner engaged a small thirty-ton vessel, the *Snapper,* to take his party and Marsden around, together with their stores. Marsden came because Turner had brought a message from Leigh, telling not only of his sickness but also of his difficulty persuading George to come to terms over the land on which the missionaries wished to settle.[63] Despite his other problems, Marsden did not hesitate to help. He must undoubtedly have felt some irritation over the Wesleyan mission. Over the years he had often tried to persuade them to leave New Zealand to the CMS, but without success.[64] He had also originally intended Whangaroa as the station for Henry Williams and had now to substitute Paihia.[65] But if he felt any irritation there was no evidence of it. Though the missionary world was thick with judgement, recrimination, and reproof, no harsh words ever appear to have passed between Leigh and Marsden. On arrival, Marsden found Leigh very ill and recommended he should return to Port Jackson for more care, comforts, and medical advice. Leigh's colleagues agreed and so he duly returned.[66]

In this phase of his life, which has generally been written up as heroic triumph, Leigh was most bitterly criticized by his immediate colleagues, few of whom thought his illness genuine. Turner, for example, later wrote that the real cause of Leigh's withdrawal was not failing health but the realization that he had neither talents nor heart for the missionary work in New Zealand, adding that White confided to him that it would be a blessing if Leigh went, for if he stayed he would only hinder their efforts.[67] They both wrote home the following year, stressing that Leigh was not fitted for service in New Zealand and, in a veiled list of Leigh's inadequacies, requested 'a zealous, active, experienced, and prudent superintendent, and if possible a person well acquainted with the principles of language, and not forgetting his constitution. . . .'[68]

Back in New South Wales, Leigh was soon involved in violent quarrels with his colleagues. Lawry, returned from Tonga, claimed Leigh had misrepresented him.[69] On 31 March 1824, at a quarterly meeting attended by Erskine, Leigh, Carvosso, Lawry, Walker, and Horton, Leigh withdrew the various charges he had made against Lawry.[70] William Walker had written a few weeks earlier: 'Mr Leigh will smile upon you while meditating the destruction of your peace',[71] and at the beginning of the year wrote that a variety of opinions were held about Leigh's illness but he had never altered his own view that 'Mr L. has something on his mind, the future consequence of which he fears and this disorders his body'; and loads of medicine and bleedings plus the excitation of his mind had merely rendered his disorder more dangerous.[72] Robert Howe, editor of the *Sydney Gazette* and a leading Methodist, also wrote, criticizing Leigh's extravagance in New Zealand, adding: 'Evidently Mr Leigh is diseased in mind, for his body appears as strong and robust as ever. He may make a supernumerary but he is no longer, if ever he was, adapted to a missionary life. Mrs Leigh is an excellent woman.'[73]

It is difficult to dismiss completely such a chorus of criticism; but Leigh's critics were themselves subject to criticism. Not only was Walker to be dismissed; Australia was described by Richard Watson as 'the only mission which has been a disgrace to us'.[74] Marsden also wrote at the beginning of 1824, that he feared Leigh would not survive, that he was much troubled by rash young colleagues spending money too freely, adding that he knew too well how difficult it was to govern young missionaries.[75] Leigh's doctor did not consider he was shamming; in February 1824 he certified he was 'seriously indisposed with chronic affection of the liver and of the abdominal viscera generally'.[76]

Before leaving Whangaroa, Marsden performed one other major task. He helped negotiate the agreement whereby the three Ngatiuru chiefs ceded land for the mission station. It is described as 'a piece or parcel of land containing fifty acres more or less, bounded on the east side by a small wood and a gully, on the west by the road made by the crew of the *Dromedary* to bring the timber to the river, and on the north by the river, and on the south by the rising ground above the present missionary house, for which land the aforesaid Rev. Samuel Leigh agrees to pay the said George two blankets, three red cloaks, and fifteen axes'. The agreement was dated 16 August and as well as being marked by the three chiefs, was signed by Leigh, Marsden, and Shepherd.[77] The following day, Marsden administered the sacrament and churched Mrs Shepherd. On the 19th they finally left, George weeping as he bade farewell to Mr and Mrs Leigh, who were accompanied by his daughter.

White was now in charge of the mission but all was not well. Turner later wrote that White was regarded as the head of the party because he had been chosen for the mission before Turner and had preceded him in New Zealand by eight weeks: 'but alas! he was not a man fit to govern, not having "power over his own spirit" '.[78] The first words of Hobbs's journal show he was chafing under White's leadership from the very beginning.[79] Leigh noted that an old chief asked him before he left, if Mr Turner was an angry man? 'I said I hoped he was not, to which he observed that was very good for they did not like angry men to live among them.'[80]

Marsden summed up his fears. He felt much for Mrs Turner, with a young child at the breast and no (white) female companion, other than a young girl. White and Turner were both young men in a trying situation and lacking experience. 'I hope they will do well and conduct themselves with patience and perseverance. Young men are apt to be too soon angry, and if they fall into this error they will often be very uneasy. They will have much to bear with from the heathens around them until they become better acquainted with their customs and manners.'[81] Turner's phrase for the party was 'all of us raw and inexperienced'.[82] The situation was certainly not what they had expected.

III: THE DEATH OF GEORGE

Shortly after Leigh had left Whangaroa, news came that he and Marsden had been wrecked in the *Brampton* in the Bay of Islands on 7 September 1823; the work of an *atua* in George's view.[1] This delayed departure gave White time to decide that he would revisit New South Wales also, in search of a wife. He sailed with Leigh and Marsden on the *Dragon* on 14 November 1823.[2] 'May he be guided by Heaven in this important affair, Amen', wrote Turner.[3]

At first sight it was strange that White should have left for such a reason after only six months in New Zealand and at a stage when the mission could ill afford the absence of a senior man. One reason must doubtless have been the predicament of Mrs Turner as sole woman, apart from 14-year-old Betsy, amid five males; a situation calling for much ribald curiosity among the mission's flock. But from later references we can assume that the perils to godly bachelordom of heathen depravity played its part; even that pillar of rectitude, John Hobbs, was approached before the year was out, by a chief with an available daughter. 'Instantly the words of my friend Pullen in Van Diemen's Land occurred to my mind: "One assaulted by a chief and his daughter with base designs cannot exclaim with indignation, 'You filthy strumpet get away' as in England without exposing himself to the danger of being killed and eaten by these wretched cannibals." '[4] Luckily for Hobbs, the very look on his face caused the chief to walk away.

During this time, as missionaries and Maoris explored each other's ideas and ways, a steady routine of existence began to evolve. Much of missionary effort was devoted to constructing mission premises. In November 1823 they began levelling

46

ground for the site of a new and permanent residence, near the first site. Turner described it as on beautiful rising ground, the gardens in a vale in front, with a stream of excellent water running through the centre.[5] The same month Hobbs took down and removed to the new site the weatherboarded four-roomed cottage that Leigh had brought from Port Jackson.[6] In December, Turner bought from George three to four acres of 'excellent land', close to their new site, for four English axes, one small hatchet, one iron kettle, and one frying pan.[7]

The tasks undertaken by Hobbs at this time show him a universal handyman: getting timber out of the wood, repairing the boat, mending the wheelbarrow, making a bench, dismantling and erecting the house, repairing a fowling piece, making a bottom for a pair of clogs, and a pair of yokes to fetch water.[8] Though Turner was engaged in activities such as fencing, his main work was gardening; and on Sunday 14 December, as Hobbs noted the following day, they came back from preaching to 'some wholesome refreshment consisting of Baked Spare Rib of Pork and some excellent green peas' grown by Turner.[9] On Christmas day, Hobbs was able to make an entry worthy of Parson Woodforde: 'This Day we were led particularly to call to mind our dearly beloved Friends in the Land of our Fathers. We dined on Turkey Ham Green Peas new potatoes and an excellent plumb pudding.'[10]

During January and February 1824, work on the house continued. Hobbs made a mould, so that Luke Wade could make bricks for a chimney,[11] and spent much of the month shingling the roof. On 22 February, Hobbs had 'the unspeakable pleasure of witnessing the Providential Return of our Dear Brother White' from New South Wales.[12] It had been a fruitless trip. His intended wife, White reported, had changed her mind, and would only marry him if he remained in the colony. Probably he could have found a suitable partner in Van Diemen's Land, but he could not spare the time. 'I feel enough on account of my situation', he wrote, 'but what can I do? if I am not deceived God and my conscience tell me that my life must be devoted to the salvation of the Heathen

. . . and therefore cannot give up the Mission either with a good conscience or a happy mind.'[13]

This was White's version. William Walker, however, wrote back that he might have taken a wife 'had he not found obstacles in his own mind. He will therefore, most probably return as he came, and be liable to ten thousand temptations of the most powerful kind, and delicate nature'. White, he said, should have been married before he came out.[14] This also was the verdict of Daniel Tyerman of the London Missionary Society in September: 'Never should a missionary go or remain among a Heathen People, without a wife, if she can live among them with safety.'[15]

All the missionaries were under mental and physical strain. Often they felt the physical exhaustion of pioneering; but as often there was the stress of coping with quick violence or behaviour which was to them unpredictable or incomprehensible. For example, when one of George's slaves drowned, White went down to the river and found a crowd of people dragging about and sporting with the dead body. He returned 'with a gloomy mind'; and a few days later, after it had been tied to a limb of a tree in the river, he presumed to annoy them, White had to make a grave and bury the putrefying body.[16] Even the normal exuberance of their neighbours upset them; Turner in particular had a low resistance to noise.

But there was also tension arising out of relations with each other, intensified by their isolation and dependence on each other. White was an especially difficult colleague, aware of his weaknesses but seemingly unable to control them. In March, for example, he wrote: 'This evening I hurt Brother T's mind very much for which I feel very sorry but it will do us both good. Oh! How the Devil desires to have us that he may sift us as wheat—may the Lord save us.'[17] Again and again he would note instances of his ill nature, his inability to control anger, wrath, and pride.[18] Anger would be succeeded by melancholy as he recorded himself 'much distressed of late with an exquisite sense of my great sinfulness in the sight of God and my unfaithfulness in his service'.[19] Often he would pass days of 'gloom and despondency', or of 'trial and temptation', and would bewail 'how time flies and I'm doing

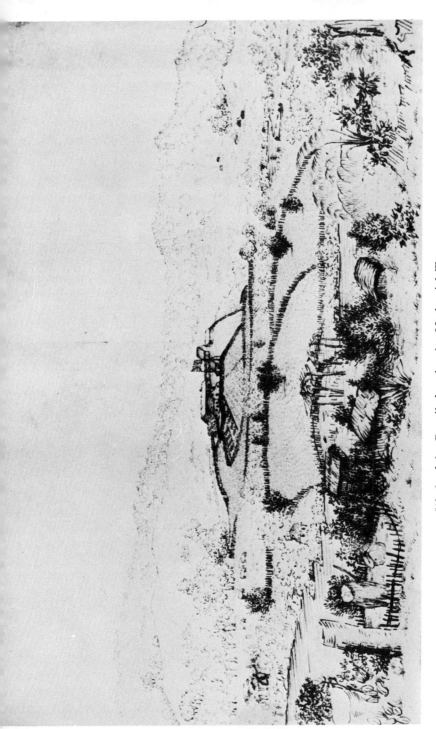

Wesleydale. Pencil drawing by Nathaniel Turner

Missionary activity in the Bay of Islands and Whangaroa, c. 1836 nothing to save the Heathen'.[20] He feared, not only that he would not be useful, but that he might be a 'hindrance in the way of others by my unchristian tempers and want of spirituality of mind'.[21]

White's spiritual turmoil has to be seen in the context of the Wesleyan belief that though he might be justified by faith, it was still possible to fall back and destroy God's influence on his life. White apparently could not answer happily the question 'Are you right with God?' However, on occasions happiness did come to him: 'I preached this morning from Gen. 5:24 and praise the Lord I felt happy in the blessed work. Oh! may I and my brethren so walk with God as to have the daily testimony that we please him that we may (if not translated) After fulfilling our day be received into his glorious presence and be forever with him to behold his Glory.'[22] There was therefore a theological explanation (whatever else there may have been) for White's extreme alternation of mood: he was with God, or he was not.

White's existence was a warfare between temperament and belief; the kind of man he was and the kind of man he believed he should be. In this the perennial problem of sex and the single missionary continued to operate. In June, after a visit from Kendall and a note in White's journal that 'I felt my mind under the influence of Powerful temptation',[23] Hobbs was told by Luke Wade of continuing reports that White had had 'unlawful connections' with Kidde, and Luke further admitted that, having heard the reports, he had been 'led astray' himself.

The same evening Hobbs spoke to Turner 'freely on the subject', and then, on Turner's advice, to White. 'Mr W. declared himself free from actual transgression though he had felt what I think need not be explained.' Next day Hobbs told Luke of White's answer, to which Luke replied, 'Well I am not.'[24] Two days later White wrote: 'Sat 19 our class meeting this evening was a peculiarly solemn and painfull *season (Poor Luke)* who has unfortunately been overcome by the flesh, was almost broken hearted and went out of the meeting weeping.'[25]

The impregnable Hobbs continued to be tested. At the beginning of 1824 a 'bestial savage' had asked him if he wanted a *wahine;* repelling the suggestion Hobbs said he had a *wahine* in Europe.[26] In June, visiting Te Pere's people, he soon had 'additional proofs of the depravity of mankind. One asked me whether I did not live in adultery with Mrs Turner —another asked me whether I was not sick with lust and another took a liberty which I was surprized at but O! how vile are those whom Satan holds in chains'.[27]

Hobbs's affections were firmly rooted in England. His journal talks of two women, Jane Broggref, who ultimately came out and married him, and a 'Mrs G.' of Broadstairs. Miss Broggref he looked on as a 'Sister in Christ'. 'This is the Birth Day of my dearly Beloved sister Jane Broggref. . . . This day my Dear Sister my prayers shall mingle with yours at a throne of Grace though you are at least 17 thousand miles distant.'[28] Mrs G., on the other hand, was 'the object of my greatest earthly delight'.[29] Twice at least he dreamt about her[30] and he noted the anniversary of the day he had left 'my worthy and beloved friend Mrs G—at Gravesend, perhaps to see her face no more but wether God sees it best for me and her to live 17 thousand miles distant or not I hope he will dispose my heart to acquiesce in his most holy and gracious will knowing that he will withhold no good thing from them that walk uprightly'.[31] As the year proceeded, Hobbs was referring to Mrs G. as his wife, as when she sent him her miniature portrait and a pair of gloves, two pencils, three quills with two pieces of ribbon and a toothbrush. By the same post 'my sister Jane' sent him *her* portrait, a watch chain and two pairs of gloves.[32]

Turner, by contrast, was clearly a happily married man. On 29 March 1824, with the aid of Mrs Fairburn of the CMS, Mrs Turner was safely delivered of a fine boy.[33] Later he was baptized Thomas by White, 'and I believe all our souls prayed Lord Seal him thine from this Hour and if it be thy will, *spare his life, Prepare him for thy work,* and send him a missionary to the Heathen', wrote Turner.[34] Mrs Turner does not figure often in Turner's correspondence; but in September he wrote that she was 'just such a partner as

my soul desired and such as I needed for a station like this',
adding that his children were healthy and likely to do well,
the eldest, a daughter born in Hobart, was beginning to
'prattle away' in Maori.[35] At the beginning of December 1824,
Luke Wade left for England, to fetch his wife;[36] and the girl
Betsy left on the *St Michael* at the end of the month.[37]

Throughout 1824 the missionaries made good progress with
construction. At the beginning of the year much effort went
into constructing buildings which could serve both as schools
and chapels at Te Puhi's village of Kaeo, and 'Udi Whare's'
village, apparently Toropapa.[38] The house at 'Udi Whare's'
was described as twenty-one feet by fifteen.[39] The buildings
had doors and windows erected by White[40] and a *raupo* roof
constructed by Te Puhi and his people, for which work they
were paid two spades, two axes, two adzes and one large
iron pot.[41] At one stage Te Puhi's enthusiasm languished and
White and Turner, comparing it with his kumara house, told
Te Puhi that the school was, in comparison, a pig-sty 'and
that we would have a better house than this for our God
on which he agreed to finish it well'.[42]

By June they were ready to open the schools, and James
Shepherd of the CMS and the Rev. Thomas Kendall came
to assist in the opening. At 10.30 a.m. on the 13th they
assembled in Te Puhi's chapel where about fifty, including
children, were present, the rest being away clearing land for
potatoes. They began singing a hymn in Maori; then Kendall
read a prayer out of his Maori grammar, White prayed in
English, and Shepherd spoke fluently in Maori. The chiefs
asked questions and Turner concluded by praying in English.
At the second chapel in the afternoon, Turner sang and
prayed and Shepherd spoke at length. The house was crowded
and many listened outside.[43]

The construction of the schools had been for months a
major undertaking; yet from the start there were difficulties
in using them as schools. One was that some form of bribery
seemed necessary to ensure attendance; yet they did not have
enough food to feed the students; and in any case, White
and Turner felt that this would lower the missionaries in the
people's estimation and discourage self-help. They quoted the

log sheet giving attendances varying from two to sixteen, with comments such as 'Most of the children away at a funeral', 'Exceedingly tried with their bad behaviour', 'Several adults at second S. very encouraging', 'Nearly all the children away looking at Mr Kendall's boat', 'Annoyed today with the vile conduct of some of the adult females'.[44] In September, visiting the schools with Stack, Turner noticed some improvement; but letters and lessons out of the Grammar were learnt parrot fashion, with little effort at understanding. However, the girl's school was doing well, especially in needlework; and he felt that though the schools were not making much progress in reading, they were 'rapidly growing in a Theoretical knowledge of the Sacred truths of Revelation'.[45]

The fact that they were erecting chapels, showed that they were following a pattern of work based on English experience; and as in England, Sunday was especially the day to visit the surrounding villages, sing and pray, exhort and dispute, after which they would return to a well-earned Sunday dinner, such as they had always known. Kaeo, especially, was frequently visited, and for all the conflicts with Te Puhi, there were times when the missionaries thought he was responding. In March, White wrote that Te Puhi and his people listened to them with remarkable attention. The old chief acknowledged that he had a bad heart and asked them to give him a new one, saying that until he knew the words of the Book he would not understand how to pray. He was anxious for his tribe and family to learn to read.[46] There are several references to an old priest in Te Puhi's village who listened to them with interest[47] and at the end of August Hobbs was encouraged by the belief that Te Puhi 'received a clear idea that our scriptures come from God'.[48]

Ngahuruhuru is an elusive figure, partly because of the wildly different missionary versions of his name; but he appears to have taken an intelligent interest in missionary teachings.[49] George was much in the missionaries' company but there is little evidence that he ever responded to their teaching.

Many other chiefs, each of whom had their own little settlement, were constantly visited. There was 'Jackey' at whose place occurred much vigorous discussion, and where at one stage they proposed to erect another school. Kearoa, whose settlement appears to have been at Whaupuke, on the way to Pupuke, was described as belonging to the missionaries' own tribe.[50] He began the year grabbing White by the neck and waving a tomahawk over him,[51] yet by September White wrote of their hope that he would be among the first fruits of the mission.[52] White and Stack visited him when he was sick; it was noted that he and his people had particularly retentive memories.[53]

Te Pere of Ngatipou was regularly visited. As well as his powerful island *pa* at the entrance to Whangaroa harbour he had a summer residence at Pupuke and he and his people were regularly visited at both places. Pupuke was described as a large settlement and the missionaries often had audiences of up to 200 there. Te Pere was described as a great chief, 'a very fine man about 50 years of age', and Turner also identified him as 'the person who took care of the *woman* and *two children* that escaped being massacred when the Boyd was cut off by the tribe with whom we now reside' and said that a separate mission to his tribe would be desirable.[54] Generally the missionaries were well received by Ngatipou, though on one occasion it was suggested they might make a *kinaki* (a tasty morsel or relish) to some turnips.[55]

Various other places were occasionally visited: 'Peppea's place', where they were working on the sabbath;[56] 'Toke's place', where they found themselves covered with lice[57] and where on another occasion George was present and wanted to talk trade rather than religion,[58] Mangaiti, where they talked to 'Eroro'; 'Duetera's place', where he and his family were not working on the Sabbath and where a child knew Christ's name.[59] Further afield they visited 'Tupe's' settlement at Wainui Bay, and also 'Matandi' (Matauri Bay?) on the way to the Bay of Islands.[60] 'Tupe' was described as having 'an uncommon quick apprehension'.[61] Oruru, to the north, which Leigh had visited, was toured by White and Shepherd in October by land[62] and in November by boat by White, Hobbs, Stack, and Luke Wade. Although the people were eager to have a missionary, and White thought the Oruru valley the most extensive, fertile, and beautiful place he had seen since coming to New Zealand, the wars of Hongi had wiped out much of the population.[63]

In between these visits the routine of pioneering went on. Hobbs continued to be the handyman, making such things as 'a Dolly for washing', a large wooden clothes horse, oars, masts, a grindstone, a bedstead for White; putting handles in spades (for George and Te Puhi) and in a hoe (for George's wife); building a fowlhouse with a privy attached; cutting and hooping a tub.[64] White described his own labours: 'working with the Axe, Spade and Saw and dragging logs of Timber through a swamp up to the knees in mud and water. It was not an uncommon thing for me to be for weeks together literally cover'd with dirt and bathed in perspiration and generally not able either to change my cloaths or to get them dry'd and in this state I have often gone to Bed which was not always a dry one and scarcely screen'd from the wind and rain and have frequently allowed my shirt to dry on my back, but in all this the Watchful care of my heavenly Father preserved my health which, to myself and others appeared little less than a Miracle'.[65]

This description of his own personal hygiene did not prevent White from commenting on the Maoris: 'They are filthy beyond description in their persons and manner of living the effluvia which arises from their persons and garments in Warm Weather together with the swarms of vermin which everywhere accompany them render our intercourse with them not quite so pleasant as it would be otherwise. It is a disgusting subject but you will bear with me when I inform you that New Zealand lice are very large and though our persons frequently swarm with them we do not find it very difficult to catch them. It is quite common for those savages to lie basking in the sun spread their garments on the ground and eat the Vermin as they catch them'.[66]

Throughout the year improvements to mission premises continued to be made. Luke Wade successfully made bricks, using the mould Hobbs had made for him; Turner burnt the lime out of cockle shells and made mortar; and White built a chimney.[67] But they still had problems. Hobbs wrote that

many of the shingles bought in New South Wales were un-
suitable.[68] In May a storm took off part of the roof, so that
the rain 'poured in in torrents'.[69] During the year they constructed a saw-pit in the bush near a stand of kauri; Hobbs
and White, in particular, toiled at this, cutting down and
dragging home the timber.[70] The hills around, wrote White,
were usually covered by fine timber, measuring from sixty to
a hundred feet clear of branches and from three to six feet
in diameter.[71]

The garden, largely Turner's responsibility, was flourishing.
Through its centre, he wrote, ran 'a never failing rill of
excellent water, which empties itself into the main river
about 100 yards below our house'. By September they were
growing beans, peas, turnips, cabbages, onions, carrots,
radishes, and several other common vegetables, together with
orange, peach, lemon, and nectarine trees, mulberry, and
vines, all of which they expected to do well. Partly assisted
by several Maoris and by James Stack and his brother Michael
who was visiting them,[72] Turner had enclosed about three
acres with a strong log fence and this they had cleared,
cultivated, and sown with wheat and barley, which they
expected would supply them with bread for a year as well
as provide food for the fowls. The soil, in Turner's view,
was of the best quality and would grow anything that grew
in England, many things better. From incidental references
it is clear that they also had cattle, as well as turkeys.[73]

As yet there was little evidence of their neighbours adopting
these new farming methods and crops. In March, White and
Turner went with George to look at his cultivated land in the
interior and found his potatoes looking well;[74] and on their
return ate a good meal of kumara with him; but in September, when Turner went into the bush to sow wheat for
the Maoris, he was grieved that they had not prepared the
ground.[75] Probably they had little incentive till they had
seen the result of Turner's own efforts.

Yet another source of food was by shooting. There are
references to shooting pigeon, duck, and pig—in pursuit
of the latter, George would often accompany White, who
appears to have been a good shot. But Turner also enjoyed

shooting, noting a danger of the pleasure of it becoming greater than the profit.[76]

It was a hard and simple life, but clearly it had its pleasures and their isolation was often broken by visitors. There was a continual interchange of visits with the CMS in the Bay of Islands. Henry Williams, John King, William Hall, James Shepherd, William Fairburn, and Thomas Kendall the former CMS missionary, all visited them at least twice during the year. There were also visits from Mrs Fairburn (to assist at Mrs Turner's lying in)[77] and from Kendall's daughter.[78] Relations between the two missionary bodies were clearly good at this stage. After a visit to Whangaroa (during which he baptized William Fairburn)[79] Henry Williams wrote to Samuel Leigh: 'It is good it is a pleasant thing for brethren to dwell together in Unity. It is like a precious ointment upon the head, it is as the dew of Hermon.'[80] Not only did the CMS preach when visiting Whangaroa, White was also asked by Henry Williams to address a meeting when in the Bay of Islands, which he did 'with unusual freedom'.[81] The only dark moment in this happy relationship was in August when a blacksmith accompanying Henry Williams seduced one of the mission girls, for which he was later 'turned away' by Williams, as was the girl herself by the Wesleyans.[82]

In addition to the CMS visits, an increasing number of ships began to visit Whangaroa, probably encouraged by the presence of the missionaries. On 22 February 1824, the schooner *Endeavour* (Captain Dacre) brought White back from New South Wales, together with a large supply of stores.[83] In July, Captain Dacre was back again, this time with the deputation from the London Missionary Society, the Rev. D. Tyerman, Mr George Bennet, and the Rev. L. G. Threkeld, a missionary from Tahiti. White visited them on board ship, in time to calm an uproar which occurred when the Captain imprudently pushed some Maoris overboard. The three missionaries came on to the station and later wrote in high commendation of what they saw.[84] The *Endeavour* and Captain Dacre came a third time in October, when there was more uproar and White complained to George about the females on board.[85]

Thomas Kendall also made several trading visits in a small cutter he owned at this time.[86] White, whose career was later to have many similarities to that of Kendall, wrote of him: 'He is *indeed* an object of pity. May the Lord restore him and make his fall a Blessing to others.'[87] In December the *St Michael* (Captain Beveridge) visited Whangaroa.[88] There were in addition occasional European visitors: not only Stack's brother Michael[89] but also, for example, Philip Tapsell, first officer of the whaler *Asp,* and a Mr Gardner, mate of the *Fanny.* Hobbs noted that Tapsell brought with him his Maori wife, 'the first Native that has undergone the Christian Matrimonial operation'.[90]

All in all, 1824 was an encouraging year; the material basis of the mission was firmly established and there was some evidence of teaching impact. The next year, however, problems began to multiply. The year began with one of those mysterious trips to the south to which White became addicted in later years. While waiting in the Bay of Islands, he wrote home that he was going in a small cutter belonging to Kendall 'to ascertain the extent of the population and the state of their minds in reference to missionaries settling amongst them'.[91] His journal describes the first part of his journey and then abruptly breaks off. There is no evidence that he reported on his expedition or that his colleagues commented in any detail, Possibly they were hoping to find a more suitable area to work in;[92] possibly the expedition had little or nothing to do with the mission and White was becoming involved in Kendall's activities. During the expedition he explored the River Thames, and later claimed to have ventured as far as Horotiu, on the Waikato River south of Ngaruawahia.[93]

While White was away, the missionaries had little encouragement. Turner was not well; at the beginning of January he wrote of 'feebly' attempting to talk and pray to the people; at the beginning of February he wrote that his mind was considerably tried: 'I feel unwell in Body and Satan thrusts hard at my soul. Lord uphold me or I fall.'[94] At the school, Turner and Stack found the boys more inclined to sleep than be instructed;[95] at the end of January, Stack wrote that the

'native schools have not been attended by me as it is found
on our present plan unlikely to do any good'. The children
in the household were disorderly; and when they went out to
preach they found that because of the heat and the 'continual
drowsiness' of their audience, it was impossible to gain their
attention.[96] On the other hand, their farming efforts were
prospering. Early in January Turner was thrashing out and
winnowing his barley, achieving 'better than 12 bushels from
a very small patch of land', which he thought would be very
useful for their fowls;[97] later in the month he thrashed and
winnowed 'about 20 bushels of good wheat' and taught
'Ahede' how to use a sickle on some wheat Turner had sowed
for him earlier.[98] Later they bought the wheat from him.[99]

At the same time as waning interest in missionary teaching,
there was internal conflict and threat from without for the
Whangaroa people. At the beginning of January there was
a quarrel between old Te Puhi and George. Stack said it was
over a pig of George's which had got into Te Puhi's kumara;[100]
but Turner, noting the considerable disturbance in the valley,
added that Te Puhi 'threatened to come and Destroy us
altogether, but with this we were not moved'.[101] This suggests
that the missionaries had a part in the ill-will between the
brothers. Later in the month there was a message that one
of George's wives was ill; Turner and Stack were told her
spirit had fled, but that she had a new spirit, 'a waidua o'
(wairua). They sent her medicine, which Turner said was
effective.[102] A few days later, George was ill, complaining of
a pain in the left shoulder blade and ribs, growing worse,
Stack thought, partly because of the state of his mind. They
did not send him a drink because he would keep the bowl;
and were treated 'with a great deal of indifference bordering
on contempt' by George's people for being the reason why
he did not get better. In the night muskets were fired to
frighten the spirits away.[103]

Associated with this internal tension was the expectation
that Patuone, the Hokianga chief, was going to attack.[104]
Going out to preach in the valley with his wife and Hobbs,
Turner could gain little response; the valley was full of noise,

as chiefs exhorted their people to be strong and not fear their enemies.[105] A message came from the Bay of Islands chief Tareha, saying that if the Hokianga people came, he would be their ally. Rumours continued throughout the month, and were accompanied by 'dancing and great noise in the valley'.[106] There was a recurrent note of bewilderment in the missionaries' writings at this point: 'Persons', wrote Hobbs, 'who are influenced by mere selfish Motives and destitute of all that is called human Honour will be found quere subjects to deal with'.[107]

Eventually the Hokianga *taua,* or war-party, of thirty canoes arrived. White, who had returned from his trip to the Thames, encountered them while sailing round with Henry Williams from the Bay of Islands. This was probably White's first meeting with Patuone and Nene, who were to be so important in the Hokianga phase of the mission. It was an amicable encounter, but the missionaries were detained lest they gave the alarm. Patuone told them they were going against a tribe at Whangaroa who had killed two of his sons in battle. White and Williams spent the time of waiting talking with various chiefs; when they left in the evening and were pulling past Te Pere's *pa,* White was asked by name if he had seen the *taua.* Keeping word with his recent captors, he made no reply and Williams replied in English.[108] The *taua* attacked Te Pere's settlement at Pupuke, destroying houses, fences, and nearly ripened corn.[109]

On arrival, White visited George, who pressed his nose several times, saying his heart was dark and he was very ill.[110] Ngahuruhuru became very upset over George's condition, crying out so that he might be heard for a long way and firing several muskets to drive away the evil spirit that had come to fetch George away to the *Po.* At the same time he also asked the missionaries to look into their books and send some medicine.[111] They sent him a dose of calomel and julep, the same sovereign remedy with which Hobbs was hoping to cure his worms. It did not have the desired effect,[112] and Stack reported George's wife complained that his drinks were not sweetened. 'On our denying the assertion as false his brother said New Zealand men were not like us that they had great throats and required a great deal of sugar to satisfy them.' Missionary medicine was decried; they were told that if George died, the Hokianga people would come and rob the missionaries: 'The reason why, who can tell?' There was little encouragement in missionary attempts at preaching; and still muskets were fired at night to drive away the God that was eating George—or was it 'a stone from another world in his bowels put in by the New Zealand God'?[113]

Daily the missionaries visited George. Despite the failure of their medicine, he asked them 'to pray to Jesus Christ to take the God out of his belly'.[114] Then the missionaries heard that George had asked a Hokianga priest to rob the mission house, saying he had not had *utu* for his father being blown up after the taking of the *Boyd*.[115]

At this stage George's wife thought he was dying; but by the following month he had recovered enough to play an active part in various tumults. The first was when his daughter injured herself and George obtained *utu* by plundering 'a poor man unable to defend himself' who had nothing to do with the accident. This was incomprehensible to Turner who commented: 'Anything will serve for an excuse when they wish to plunder.'[116]

The following day there was a dispute over the price to be paid for one of the puppies of the missionaries' bitch Rose. Ngahuruhuru offered 'a very indifferent pig', which was refused. He went off, then returned and broke in, for which he was reproved by White. At the same time his son, young Te Puhi, had engineered the theft of one of the puppies. In an ensuing scuffle involving White, the details of which are not altogether clear, Turner was struck a blow with a broken spear by young Te Puhi. George came, firing off his gun; and Turner was put to bed with the inevitable dose of salts, his whole frame 'seriously injured from the shock'.[117]

Hardly had this uproar subsided than news arrived that Ngatipou were plundering a ship, the *Mercury* (Captain Edwards), of London, at the heads. They were after the powder and muskets, of which they must have been in particular need after the recent attack by the Hokianga *taua*.

White and Stack went down with old Te Puhi in an attempt to mediate. For a while they restored order; then trouble broke out again and Captain and crew abandoned the ship, which was now skilfully plundered. While the Captain waited outside the harbour, White went back to try and make peace. Eventually the ship was surrendered to him and he left Stack and Te Puhi on board as guardians overnight while he went back to the mission station to fetch a quadrant—a somewhat alarming experience for Stack. The next day, with the aid of the ship's mate and two crew members, White and Stack attempted to take the ship out of the harbour, only to be blown away in the direction of the North Cape, fifteen or twenty miles N.E. of which they finally had to abandon the vessel. After an alarming night ashore among hostile Maoris, who stole what they could, the party reached home on 9 March 1825.[118]

The *Mercury* affair left trouble in its wake, not only for Ngatipou but for Ngatiuru also. First there was the danger of European reprisal; or failing this that Hongi or others would take vengeance for threatening their supply of European weapons. There was also the danger that no more European vessels would visit Whangaroa.[119] Finally, there was the danger that the missionaries themselves would withdraw. On 18 March Turner took his pregnant wife and two children to Kerikeri; and for a while there were continual discussions between the Wesleyans and the CMS over whether the Whangaroa station should be abandoned.

Though there were strong reasons for staying, there were also powerful reasons for withdrawal. The Whangaroa people had behaved badly to the missionaries; they had attacked the *Mercury*, thus provoking a Maori punitive expedition, in the wake of which the mission station was likely to be endangered. By staying among such a people, the Wesleyans might be encouraging similar behaviour against the CMS. Finally, George's request that the Hokianga people should exact *utu* from the missionaries if he died, had also to be taken into account.[120]

During March a war party headed by Rangituke from Paihia and Waikato of Rangihoua did in fact set out to punish the Whangaroa people and to remove the Wesleyan missionaries and their property, for which purpose Rangituke had a canoe seventy feet long and seven feet wide. On their way they stopped near John King's station; but one of their party falling ill after a breach of *tapu*, they lost heart. On the 24th the party dispersed and King was able to let loose his sheep, goats, and fowls.[121]

For the moment the threat passed; but nobody knew whether Hongi would still restrain those Bay of Islands chiefs who wished to destroy the Whangaroa people. Turner at this time was travelling between his family at Kerikeri and his colleagues at Whangaroa; and he began to consider quitting. His wife's health was much impaired and he feared for her life. He hoped her removal to the Bay of Islands would be a help but doubted whether she should return to being the sole woman on the Whangaroa mission. His children had recovered but his own health, he wrote, was 'on the Decline, and I have my fears will not be able to stand the noises and trials of N.Z. land long. My nervous system is so affected that at times I scarce know what to do with myself' adding that he thought that if the Society knew the situation they would think of removing him to one of the colonies.[122] Towards the end of March he recorded his 'great depression of spirit and uneasiness of soul chiefly arising from a deep sense of my little spirituality of Mind, and want of better qualifications for the great work of Evangelising the Heathen'. Going over the hills with Hobbs he found he could scarcely talk to the people at all.[123]

At the same time, George continued to decline, probably with the unintentional assistance of missionary medical efforts. One evening, wrote Stack, a messenger came with news that he was dead. White went down and found the old priest Atahahu calling back George's spirit from the invisible world. 'He had taken some opening medicine at noon and perhaps it was the effect of it on his weak frame that produced a weakness. The groans of his wife could be heard from our house.' Two days later she came asking Stack to make him a pancake and to provide sweeter tea; a request which Stack thought unreasonable.[124]

Stack also learnt from the boys at the mission house that George was in fact dying of 'the bewitching art of his sister in law', who was of a tribe of priests and was turning her skill against him because he had beaten his wife. There was, Stack learnt, a difference between death by witchcraft, where a necromancer went to a swamp, made a canoe out of bulrushes and set it sailing, muttering something mysterious at the same time; and natural death, which was when a spirit returned after death and, wishing someone to be with him, attacked him with disease, which they called being eaten inside by their gods.[125] Whatever the cause of his illness, Hobbs, when visiting him, noted that his flesh was quite wasted away.[126]

Again there was a threat of Bay of Islands attack, which receded when the party, having reached Matauri, ate some food cooked in a sacred oven and, going to sea, had one of their canoes upset by a *taniwha,* at which they all returned home, though an attack was still promised for a few months' time.[127] A few days after this release, the people of the valley held the ceremony of crying over bones taken from the sacred sepulchres, in which they were joined by Ngatipou. Te Puhi asked the missionaries to come, wearing their best clothes; they came, observing about seven skulls placed in line and anointed with turkey feathers. But instead of a solemn ceremony it was an occasion of 'laughter and folly' in Hobbs's view, with the chief person delivering speeches in, Hobbs thought, 'the most trifling and nonsensical manner'. The missionaries attempted to preach about the Resurrection, but without success.[128]

The next day there was great mirth in the valley over Te Pere's arrival; and the missionaries' servant David had 'illicit commerce' with a beautiful young woman, as a result of which three men were waiting to kill him.[129] Rival parties assembled around the mission house; Te Puhi fired a musket over their heads and David fled for safety.[130]

Such continued disorder kept alive the missionary wish to withdraw. However, there was one major obstacle, the amount of time and money which had been spent on the mission buildings and the amount of trade and other goods which might be lost by premature flight. During April 1825, White was making successive journeys to the Bay of Islands, secretly removing whatever items he could, at considerable risk in overloaded boats, while old Te Puhi would call in, anxiously checking on what had disappeared. He refused to lend a canoe to send wheat and pork to Turner.[131]

As the weeks passed, more and more items were removed. This, in itself, was a reason for delaying the move. There was also the fear that they might be killed in the act of moving; that removal might provoke more hostilities between Whangaroa and the Bay of Islands, or an attack on the next European vessel to visit Whangaroa. There was also a possibility at this stage that the Leighs might be returning from New South Wales.[132] But though they delayed the move, it was assumed that the mission would be abandoned. White talked of removing to New South Wales before resuming elsewhere in New Zealand, but only when they had a full complement; and he mentioned his own desire to return to England 'to obtain a suitable partner'.[133]

On 17 April, Hobbs and White went to see George. By then he was almost a skeleton; and reflecting on his imminent death, Hobbs feared that when he appeared before the judge of all the earth, he would receive the sentence: 'Depart from me thou cursed into everlasting fire prepared for the Devil and his Angels.' Destitute of all knowledge which would make salvation possible, George had said when in health: 'I do not wish to hear about Jesus Christ I wish to hear about Tommyhawks etc.'[134]

That evening at 7 o'clock, a great cry went up in the valley and the missionaries knew that George was dead. All Maoris on the station immediately fled to the village to hide; the missionaries themselves, locking up the station, hastened up the hill to hide. Here they listened and debated what to do, whether to flee by night to Kerikeri, whether to follow the Apostolic example of 'praying to the Lord and casting lots', to decide what to do. At length, as nothing happened, they ventured back to the mission station, still prepared for flight.

'George, second in rank to the
New Zealand King Tabooha'
Watercolour by Samuel Leigh, 1823

'The New Zealand King Tabooha'
Watercolour by Samuel Leigh, 1823

They listened to the noise. George was being removed to the *wahi tapu*. Ngahuruhuru was making a great outcry but they could not guess its meaning. Gradually their fears subsided and they committed themsleves to God. Finally a message came that old Te Puhi wanted two of them to take a light and go to the *wahi tapu*. White went alone, and soon returned, having been kindly received.

So, shortly after midnight, they went to bed and enjoyed, wrote Stack, 'on the whole a good night's repose'. He reflected on the fact that a few months back, George had been lively and active, unequalled in strength by any Maori in the valley.[135] The next day White viewed the body again: his account, wrote Stack, 'was rather disgusting than interesting. Men and women of the richer sort generally crying and cutting themselves with stones till the blood flowed profusely whilst the excrements of the nose were suffered to remain hanging in icicles as it were to give full proof of the sincerity of their grief'.[136]

Hobbs was asked to make a box to take George's body in a sitting position. He measured him and then worked all day, making it of the dimensions two feet six inches wide, three feet six inches long, three feet high; and White painted it red. When he took it to them in the evening, wrote Hobbs, 'it gave them much satisfaction because it would allow of his sitting in a natural and easy manner instead of lying straight as Europeans do which some who have been to Port Jackson and seen our manner do not approve'.[137]

The large red box was placed prominently on the large sugar-loaf hill in the middle of the valley, 'which the natives called the pa', and it could be seen a long way off. Ngatipou came to pay their respects and walked up the hill, firing off their muskets as they went. Then they sang the *pihe,* or funeral ode. The missionaries, who had feared they might be plundered by Ngatipou, were relieved they were not molested. The same day Turner, in much anxiety for the safety of his friends, arrived from Kerikeri.[138]

Very little of significance happened the next few months, but gradually the tension subsided. There were reports that six hundred Maoris were coming from Hokianga to carry out

George's instructions, which were variously interpreted as to plunder the missionaries, or to kill first the missionaries then the inhabitants of the valley. Te Puhi warned them not to give the Hokianga people the powder the missionaries had stored for George. White asked him to take it away, which he did; and when the Hokianga people came on 2 May they were peaceful.[139] There were continual rumours of Hongi's war in the Kaipara and of his intentions with regard to Whangaroa on his return. But as yet nothing happened. Turner commuted between the Bay of Island and Whangaroa, despite ill-health; and at Kerikeri on 4 May his wife, 'highly favoured in the Hour of Nature's sorrow', was safely delivered of a son.[140]

There appeared to be little attempt to preach in this period. Turner at Kerikeri was reading 'Campbell's Travels' and accounts from the Sandwich Islands (Hawaii) in the American *Missionary Herald;*[141] at Whangaroa his colleagues read sermons on appropriate subjects, such as 'Daniel in the Lion's Den'[142] and studied the language. Hobbs even attempted to translate the Lord's Prayer, portions of scripture and the catechism.[143] White, talking to a Bay of Islander, learnt of George's 'secret duplicity' (unspecified) towards them before his death; and also that Te Puhi had formerly behaved badly towards the missionaries because they had treated George as the principal chief, 'which honour did not belong to him but to Tepuhee who would now treat us well', wrote Stack.[144]

News came of George, now apparently not where the missionaries had mentally assigned him, but where he had a fine *pu* and was carried in the arms of a numerous body of Maoris who 'out of respect would not suffer him to walk'.[145] Ngahuruhuru was less blessed in this world when Hobbs refused to mend his musket.[146] He had apparently concluded that the missionaries' God had killed George.

Towards the end of May it appeared as if the missionaries might be re-establishing influence. Turner on a visit to Whangaroa recorded that they went out preaching on the Sunday and all were now well disposed: there were reports of ships in the Bay of Islands and the Maoris were afraid these were coming round to kill them. Stack also thought the behaviour of local people had improved, though there had been instances with the sick where 'a mean spirit of dependency' had been shown. 'We need much wisdom in attempting to do them good lest we hurt ourselves and them also. They are such unreasonable creatures.'[147]

There was other evidence of a return of missionary confidence. At the beginning of June, Turner was putting in a week's labour at the farm and garden and on 8 June they all decided to build bedrooms and a room in which to cook and live, for White, Hobbs, and Stack. The existing house would accommodate the stores and Turner's family, with a spare room for visitors.[148] Towards the end of the month, stores arrived in the Bay of Islands for the mission. Turner arranged to have them transported to Kerikeri but then decided that if they could risk their lives at Whangaroa they could risk their stores.[149] A few days later he brought his family back to Whangaroa, his three children being carried by two girls and three boys. Mrs Turner, sitting in a chair with a pole fastened on each side, was carried by four men.[150] The following day the *Industry* arrived with White in the harbour and the next few days were spent unloading stores.[151] At the end of the month the half-yearly return of trade showed that supplies were back to normal.[152] They were all at their post and ready to try again.

IV: 'DREADFUL DEPRAVITY'

In this period, John Hobbs became more influential. His was a mixed contribution. He lacked the inspirational qualities which White brought to tasks of leadership; but he was less erratic and moody. He lacked Turner's qualities as a conciliator; but he had greater physical resilience in the face of violence and noise. He was an uncomfortable colleague, not backward in administering reproof; but he was a source of stability whose practical talents were essential. Thus although White at first told Hobbs he could not labour with him because they could never agree on official business, on further reflection he told him he would work with him.[1] Such passages occur from time to time in Hobbs's journal and suggest there was always latent hostility between them. But Hobbs was not to be gainsaid and the minutes of the Methodist Conference of 1824 recorded his acceptance as a missionary.[2] Stack, on the other hand, while contributing much as a linguist and teacher, does not appear to have tried to influence his colleagues greatly. He was not physically strong. He wrote of his pleasure at helping Turner sow wheat, 'owing to the healthy influence the open air has on my sickly frame'. The Maoris, he said, called him *Tuai,* meaning sickly.[3]

For a while the hints of progress which had encouraged the return of Turner's family continued. For example, young Te Puhi, who had attempted to spear Turner, asked to be reconciled with him. He gave Turner a pig and Mrs Turner a fine mat and in return was given a hoe; and the two men shook hands and rubbed noses.[4] At the end of July the missionaries increased the number of children living with them, including two sons and a daughter of old Te Puhi; and they decided that as soon as a chimney was added to an outbuilding and an apartment added to it as a store room for casks, a vigorous effort would be made, not only with these children, but also among the villages.[5] Confidence restored, they were trying the old methods again.

At the same time they still had to live amid intermittent violence. On 17 June, as a satisfaction for the death of George, the daughter of a person much disliked by him was speared in the head and brought to the missionaries for treatment. 'Their superstitions', wrote Hobbs, 'are indeed truly mysterious and many of their actions unaccountable.'[6] A month later, the missionaries' Sunday service was interrupted with the news that a fighting party from Oruru had speared two children as *utu* for George's death. When the missionaries rose from their knees and ran out to see what was happening, they were alarmed to see a band of naked men with spears, rushing at them as if to despatch them at once; but at a call from Ngahuruhuru they stopped. Turner wrote that he felt shocked for the rest of the day and his wife's nerves were considerably shaken.[7]

Hardly had they recovered from this alarm when there was a visit from Hongi and from Ngatihao, the tribe of Patuone and Nene in the Waihou district of the Hokianga. For days before, there was confusion and noise; pigs were caught, some taken to the *pa* in readiness for the attack, others sold to the missionaries in exchange for iron pots for cooking and for holding water if besieged. Turner was told the visitors would eat the people of the valley for breakfast, those at the heads of the harbour for dinner, those of the North Cape for supper, and still not be satisfied. Kemp and Clarke at Kerikeri wrote that the tribes from Waimate and the Bay were coming over to have satisfaction for the taking of the *Mercury;* but if their taking of pigs and potatoes was not opposed they would not kill anyone, nor did they intend to molest the missionaries.[8]

Although Ngatiuru assembled with their possessions on the north and north-west side of the hill *pa,* they made no fortifications, which suggests the significance of the *pa* was ritual rather than military. First came Ngatihao, who were on the side of the Ngatiuru, pilfering what they could from the mission; then on 23 July 1825 the Ngapuhi came, performing a *haka* at the foot of the *pa,* levelling a building belonging to Te Puhi, or going through the valley plundering. Hongi called on the missionaries with his two wives and two children. He was fed on pork and rice, but because he was *tapu* because of the death of his son, he ate outside and was fed by another son, 'Port Jackson'. Both Hongi and the chief Tareha, one of the stoutest men he ever saw, wrote Turner,[9] were given a blanket each, and lesser chiefs, with some reluctance, were given hatchets. Hongi placed a *rahui* on the missionaries' wheat field; but this did not prove very effective; and for the next few days the missionaries were on a twenty-four-hour watch, in a vain attempt to prevent pilfering by 'these children of Belial who like a swarm of bees had now come up and covered the country', as Stack put it. The boat house was pilfered; even the silk handker-chief in Turner's pocket was filched when he went out. All the time there were demands for food; to avoid feeding every-one, they went without food themselves, or cooked at night; on one occasion Tareha, finding no food ready, stretched his great body on the floor and slept.

Hongi and Te Puhi had a friendly interview; but Ngatipou refused to come and negotiate; and as Hongi was not well, he left, burning his camp before leaving. 'Our poor natives', wrote Stack, 'look like men who have been delivered from the sentence of death.'[10]

For all this, the ensuing months showed that Hongi's visit and departure had in no way removed their fears and un-certainty. On 12 August there was again much shrieking and noise and the missionaries feared it was the Bay of Islanders with murderous intent. However, it was a Hokianga tribe, under the *tohunga* Hauhau, their garments all red with *kokowai* (red ochre) come to remove George's bones and to persuade Te Puhi to remove to the Hokianga for safety. Te Puhi, who knew that a chief 'of considerable reputation' was still intending to attack him, was for a while persuaded. He warned the missionaries that in a future attack they could expect more trouble than on Hongi's visit.[11]

On 15 August, Turner and Stack went to Kaeo to observe

the removal of George's body from the red box on the hill. They described the body as in a sitting posture, entirely covered up tight with 'Tappa or Oteheitan cloth', richly dressed with oil and red ochre, the top of the head covered with turkey feathers. Te Puhi, who was building a little shed over the body, told the missionaries that their red box was a bad thing: it was too hot and the flesh did not dry and waste away as it did when exposed to the air. 'We judged by this', wrote Stack, 'that the body must be in a very offensive state.' Even in death, it seemed, the Europeans were a plague on George. Turner did not like the speeches, which he described as 'altogether Frothy and Filthy'; and he thought Te Puhi's attention to his brother's body 'little less than Idol worship'. There was much taunting between the two tribes and Ngahuruhuru said: 'Am I to go away from here? No I shall not.'[12]

The following day, Te Puhi's wife, who was related to Hongi, returned from the Bay of Islands where she had been to see him. She assured them that the Bay of Islands people were not hostile.[13] Te Puhi himself consolidated this by going to Waimate later in the month to cry over the bones of Hongi's son 'Charley', who had been killed at Kaipara.[14] It was perhaps the more expedient for Te Puhi to show good-will, because George's widow was the daughter of the principal chief of Kaipara.[15]

There continued to be indications of social tension. Stack, visiting a tribe, probably 'Jackey's', described several cases of disease: a chief's daughter affected with 'a sort of leprous scrofula', her arms and legs quite wasted, and in pain from hard swollen tumours; a boy wasting away from 'a consumption'. An old man called out 'and asked why the (atua) or God was afflicting them in this kind of way. He is destroying our tribe said he'.[16] Stack noticed many of 'our Natives' had had themselves tattooed 'that they might look frightful to their enemies'. He told one of them that Jehovah was angry at such work, receiving the reply that it was a very good thing to them. 'From this subject', wrote Stack, 'he passed to make remarks on our noses which he said were not good they projected out too much and in rubbing noses (New Zealand salutation) the forehead could not touch like they could with flat ones.' Stack noted that to signify their disapproval of the 'wilful' self torture of tattooing, the missionaries would do nothing to relieve the pain involved.[17]

Although such hints of what was going on in the minds of the people around them were not promising, the missionaries continued with their routine and there was even a note of optimism in their despatches. 'We are still at our Post', wrote Turner in September, 'with our Hearts I trust in our work and a prospect of success before us.'[18] First there was the routine of farming. By the end of July, Turner had sowed about three acres of wheat, which he reckoned was sufficient to supply the family with bread.[19] On 9 August, one of the cows calved, the first such occasion at Wesleydale, an event arousing much interest.[20] Turner looked on it as 'a grateful circumstance', as they would now have plenty of milk and butter; and at the same time ('Praise the Lord for Temporal mercies') a fine piece of fresh beef arrived from the Bay of Islands.[21] At the end of August and in September, Turner was out sowing wheat for the Maoris.[22] At the same time, work on the mission premises continued; the fences were repaired and when the attempt to burn shells in a kiln, for lime, was unsuccessful, they tried building the kitchen chimney with clay and sand as mortar.[23]

As the material basis of the mission was consolidated, a request for stores in September gave an indication of their way of life and of their ambitions for the future. While requesting to be allowed to live in separate families, they asked for a good large bell, a vice, equipment for a forge, handsaw files, a plough, a pair of smith's screwing stocks, a strong wrench, twelve strong latches for gates, a patent corn mill, two wheat riddles, a dozen milk pans, two pairs of milk strainers, a copper boiler, a coffee pot, a teapot, two pairs of bellows for each family, one brass chamber pot each, basins, pots, kitchen tongs, beds and bedding, 100 pounds of shot for ducks and pigeons, good blankets for trade, clothing for 'native' boys and girls, a printing press, and stationery.[24]

There are not many references to itinerant Sunday

preaching in the latter part of 1825; it still went on, but accounts of the response—that attention was paid, or a hope that all was not in vain—are fairly cautious. Part of the trouble, as Stack indicated, was that for all the time they had been in New Zealand they could still 'hardly say anything as we would wish'; however, some of the boys and girls they were teaching were promising, and there was a reasonable hope that if converted they would become effective 'Heralds of salvation' to their countrymen.[25] About this time it was decided they would each take one of the boys in the household, as an assistant, in the hope that they could instruct them more effectively. Hobbs took a fifteen-year-old boy, named Ika (or Hika), whom they all thought promising; he was, in fact, to be the first person baptized by the Wesleyan mission several years later. Stack, who did most of the teaching of boys in the household, recorded Hika's delight over the doctrine of the atonement.[26] Much time was spent teaching the boys and girls to sing and Turner expressed pleasure at their improvement.[27] However, even here there were disappointments. A girl, 'Shadi', who had been with them for two years, was taken away by her relatives and given in marriage to a twelve-year-old boy with whom she did not wish to live.[28] A few weeks later, she was round the mission station again, 'as dirty and filthy as the rest of the natives instead of clean garments . . . now dressed in a matt daub'd with red ochre and oil and her face blacked'.[29]

Now that the mission seemed to be settling back into its normal routine, neither White nor Turner said any more about leaving. Suddenly, however, to their great surprise, Hobbs formally presented them, on 8 September 1825, with a letter expressing his desire to return to England by a vessel currently in the Bay of Islands. He gave as his reasons that the frailty of his constitution rendered him an unfit person to be a missionary, that his preaching abilities were inadequate, that it would be improper for him to remain in New Zealand unmarried and that the way was not open for him to obtain a wife.[30]

Turner wrote that the letter caused him much grief and surprise. It was 'a trick of the Devil' to get Hobbs away.

Hobbs, he felt, was well qualified for missionary work and in some respects had superior talents; his constitution, though not of the strongest, was far from weak and he was much better since he came to New Zealand. His preaching wanted only practice. However, Turner agreed it would be improper for Hobbs to remain in New Zealand without a wife, any longer than necessary.[31] 'Matrimonial concerns' were in fact the basis of Hobbs's restlessness. He had learnt from his mother that Jane Broggref was willing to come out and marry him, or to marry him in England.[32]

From the surviving documents it is impossible to reconstruct the discussion that ensued. It produced the surprising conclusion that instead of Hobbs returning, White should go, on his own responsibility. Turner, however, wrote in support. He was aware that this was contrary to the committee's instructions, yet he could not disapprove. He feared for his own wife, that she would sink under the burden of being the sole woman on the mission. As for White, he knew he would never be happy in the land without a wife:

> The committee cannot but be sensible, that the Danger to which single men are exposed to in this land from Temptation to Native Females is *Great,* but they can form but an Imperfect Idea of this, without they come and live amongst them themselves as single young men.
>
> It is a matter of unspeakable gratitude that hitherto my Brethren stand clear on this ground. But they have not been without many a Temptation, and Temptation such as has at times, led me to *Tremble* for their *Fate.* This is another reason why I cannot Disapprove of my Brother's going Home and going home by this conveyance.
>
> For in reference to the *above* as an Individual I shall be freed from many fears. For myself I cannot but believe that he missed His Providential way in coming to NZL without a wife, whatever he may do in going home to seek one.[33]

White's decision to return blocked Hobbs's chances of doing so; for though the committee might be persuaded to accept the return of one man against instructions, they would hardly condone the return of two bachelors in distress, fleeing the seductive sirens of the Southern Seas. Hobbs was by no means happy about White's decision, although he accepted White's offer of assistance in negotiating the emigration of his intended wife.[34] He took off for the Bay of Islands, where Henry Williams tried, unsuccessfully, to engage his assistance in building a schooner, in return for the assistance given earlier by the CMS in the setting up of the Whangaroa mission.[35] Hobbs did not return till a fortnight later, when he brought news that White had sailed for England.[36]

As he recorded this, Turner noted another event of some significance in New Zealand missionary history, the death-bed baptism of Christian Rangi by Henry Williams. 'Praise the Lord for one soul as a kind of first fruits from among the Thousands of this savage race. O may the great Harvest soon follow. Amen.'[37] But as yet there was little sign of any harvest at Whangaroa. At the end of the year, Turner and Hobbs carefully expressed the lack of progress as optimistically as they could: 'that though nothing like a change of heart has yet appeared amongst them divine Truth is stealing an influence on their minds though it is to them imperceptible. . . . On some occasions we feel much encouraged and at other times their extreme indifference and carelessness caused us to return with a heavy heart.'[38]

They still placed emphasis on preaching, though they were much more aware of the difficulties created by their inadequate command of Maori.[39] They began to see more promise in using the young Maoris, who lived with them on the station, to convey the missionary message to their fellow countrymen. They were taught reading and writing and to sing hymns and now accompanied the missionaries on their preaching outings to demonstrate these skills.[40] Hitherto they had used hymns in Maori written by James Shepherd of the CMS, but now Hobbs had begun writing hymns in Maori too.[41]

Although George was dead, he still lived in the minds of his people and so influenced the missionary task. For not only had his death thrown the Ngatiuru leadership off balance, it had also sharpened the conflict between the missionary and Maori explanation of man's fate after death.

In discussion with the household boys, Stack learnt that George had been carried, box and all, by a boat's crew of H.M.S. *Dromedary* on board their vessel, where he obtained a cure. He then went on shore to his father 'Pepi' and told him he had come away from this world because Te Puhi was angry with him and refused to give him a musket. To this, Stack replied that he feared George was now 'burning in that Gloomy prison "where Hope never comes". . . . I endeavoured to avoid saying what I did in such a way as to stir up an improper feeling in the native mind. For I have been frequently asked where George is now; as though with a design to see if I should say he was in Hell'.[42]

That the missionaries were becoming more circumspect in their use of hell-fire threats was a significant shift in their approach; but the frequent questioning about George's fate suggests that the Maoris were half convinced and certainly fascinated by an idea which must at the same time have been highly repellant. Perhaps of greater significance was the fact that all Maori accounts of George's fate showed him enjoying some aspect of European life. Te Puhi reported, with great seriousness, wrote Turner, that George had three European wives—the women who had been on the *Boyd* when it had been cut off some sixteen years earlier. The news had been brought by a woman who said she had been to the *Po* and seen it, at which news George's people held a *tangi nui,* or great cry.[43]

But this dependence on the European was not simply at the subconscious level; it was being felt in all manner of ways, some of which must have been exceedingly irritating. Stack told how Ngahuruhuru, accompanied by young Te Puhi and another son, came in by the cowyard gate, instead of knocking at the proper door. Taking him out his breakfast, Turner told him how 'displeased' he was that he had come in that gate. Ngahuruhuru walked off and raged; but by now all he could do was throw sticks at 'poor Rose our faithful dog' and abuse the Maori children of the household for eating flour. Following the destruction of crops in recent raids, Te Puhi and Ngahuruhuru were being fed by the missionaries, and Stack wrote that Te Puhi confessed that 'he acted very meanly in his dependance upon us. He made use of the word *peo* a term the New Zealanders apply to persons standing over others while they are eating in order to get some food. . . .' He thought that the chiefs would not thank the missionaries to live among them if they brought only the instruction and support of their children.[44]

But however humiliating it was for chiefs to live off the food brought out to them by condescending missionaries, they were at least fortunate not to be starving as many of the children were at this time. Stack, who every evening was on duty giving out food and medicine to the sick, reported a chief's wife bringing in a girl, aged about nine, who a few weeks earlier had been healthy and was now a mere skeleton. The children, he said, suffered most in lean times; for though an adult might eat fern root, a child, when weak, could not digest it. 'And this', he added, 'may be a great cause why our school children are so content. It is to be feared a plentiful harvest may thin our numbers for they love the bread of idleness.'[45]

All discussions tended to come back to the compelling hunger. When visiting a chief who pretended sickness to obtain food, Stack told the bystanders, 'there was no other God but Jehovah who made us all from one stock. Takka said "all have not the same food, Europeans have good food". "Ah, (said his wife) New Zealanders have nothing but this hard fern root to eat which is the reason they get sick." '[46]

Unfortunately there is little detail of the sickness prevalent at this time. There are references to consumption, scrofula, the dizziness the Maoris called the *turore,* malnutrition in children, and at the end of the year a fever which seemed to affect members of the missionary household worse than others.[47] Apart from consumption, none of these appear to have been directly of European origin: and although missionary medicine was gaining in prestige it was not particularly successful, as indeed the references to 'blisters' and purges would lead one to expect. As Turner commented once: 'Visited several who are sick and their case is truly pitiable, but alas, it is ours to weep over the Miseries we cannot heal.'[48]

Despite their better food and hygiene, the missionaries themselves were often sick. At the end of October, Turner noted that he and his wife were very unwell, while 'Bro Hobbs is scarce able to bear up under the feebleness of his frame'.[49] A few days later, having taken a dose of rhubarb, Hobbs 'voided' a dead worm more than a foot long and the next day was taking 'lime water and vermifuge' to get rid of his worms.[50] At the end of November Turner told the others he had an impression he would soon 'meet with sudden departure to the world of spirits', and both his wife and Hobbs had the same impression about him.[51]

Then, Mrs Turner, who was again pregnant, suffered from a racking cough. Turner, who now feared she would die, was up most nights nursing her. In this crisis they had recourse to their usual treatment, 'opening medicine' and a blister applied to the chest. Thereupon she suffered a miscarriage, and, writing post-haste for aid from the CMS, Hobbs wrote of a circumstance 'the particulars of which Brother T. is more qualified to communicate than I am I allude to that of untimely childbirth and she is now exceedingly low and unwell'.

Realizing that Mrs Turner was the only European woman on the station, the CMS immediately sent over Henry Williams and George Clarke, together with a ship's surgeon, Dr Gilmore, so drenched with rain on the journey that they did not bother to cross rivers on Maoris' backs. Later Mr and Mrs Fairburn came by whaleboat. 'This', wrote Turner, 'was kindness such as I had not expected and almost more than I could bear.'

Dr Gilmore stayed on for several days and gave them 'considerable Medical Information by which I trust we shall profit', wrote Turner. Perhaps the doctor felt they needed it. Under his treatment Mrs Turner began to recover; and on New Year's eve, bolstered up in bed, was able to join in their devotions. Mrs Fairburn stayed until 2 January 1826.[52]

It is an interesting sidelight on missionary attitudes to Maoris and to their own wives, that although Maoris must have known far more than Turner or his colleagues about the processes of childbirth, there is no indication then or later that they were ever asked for help or advice.

But as the year 1825 drew to an end, the Maoris had trouble enough of their own; so much so that old Te Puhi said that if the *Mercury* had not been robbed, he would move to Norfolk Island.[53] There was not only disease and the malnutrition following the destruction of their crops, there was also the troublesome Hongi, who, strong enough to be a dangerous enemy, was yet meeting such difficulties against the tribes to the South, he was now a dangerous man to support.

To avenge the death of his son, Hongi was preparing, once his kumara were planted, to go against the Kaipara people again; and he wanted the support of Te Puhi.[54] At the end of October he paid another visit to Kaeo, to persuade Te Puhi to join him and also, having lost most of his war canoes on his previous expedition, to obtain a boat taken from the *Mercury*. The missionaries fed him but refused to lend materials to repair the boat and tried to dissuade him from further war.[55] On another occasion, they met Hongi, and the scene as described by Stack, was very like the famous painting by Augustus Earle a few years later: Hongi sitting on the bare ground under a few boughs stuck in the ground, a few feathers stuck in his hair and wearing a European blanket; around him his chiefs and a few slaves, pounding fern root and roasting fish.[56]

Hongi's visit greatly upset George's widow, whose father was the principal chief of Kaipara; neglecting her own health she also, by neglect, caused the death of her newly born child.[57] But after Hongi had left, taking the *Mercury* boat with him, the missionaries were pleased to learn from Te Puhi that nobody, except perhaps young Te Puhi, planned to accompany Hongi. But they were still afraid. 'Tepui said Sh'ongi would kill the people at Kai parra; then go to the North Cape and kill them there and afterwards perhaps come to this valley also.' The threat of disaster hung over them and missionary reference to what God had done in bringing peace to Tahiti cannot have been very consoling.[58] Later in November, Turner and Hobbs visited the village on Sunday morning. They found Te Puhi and Ngahuruhuru basking in the sun. A message had come from Hongi, calling on them to accompany him against Kaipara. Still they answered no, pleading that most of them were ill; and still they feared that on their return the Bay of Islanders would come and kill them for the refusal.[59]

While this situation was slowly building up at Whangaroa, William White was slowly travelling to England. It was not a happy voyage, agonizing over the sins of the crew, his own want of zeal for their souls, his own seemingly wasted life. He read all of Wesley's journals. He made a chest for the Captain. Five hundred miles from land a 'pretty little bird' alighted on the ship; he made a cage for it but the bird died. Passing the Azores, a sailor was washed overboard 'gone into Eternity, in the midst of his wickedness', unsaved by White. Finally, on 11 February 1826, four years after he and the Turners had left Deal for New Zealand, Land's End was seen off the quarter deck, twenty weeks and five days after leaving the Bay of Islands.[60]

Two days later, at about the time that Hobbs was writing yet another appeal for married help,[61] White, having preached to 'the poor sailors' from 'The end of all things is at hand etc' went ashore with his Maori companion 'Shukey', and took coach for Ramsgate, where in no time he was involved in the Hobbs circle. 'They instantly hurried me into a respectable shop just opposite and conducted me into the kitchen. In a few moments the confusion occasioned by the surprise of so unexpected a person subsided. The master of the house said "My name is Weller", and pointing to the opposite side of the room said "That is Mrs W. and that is Miss Broggref her sister". News flew as swift as wind and in a short time Mr and Mrs Hobbs and one of their daughters came to Mr Weller. The evening drew on and arrangements were made for us to go to Margate to a love feast. A most precious time after which we took supper at a Mr Cobbes.'[62]

White still had to appease his committee over his un-authorized return. Many, wrote Secretary Morley later, were

'Hongi and Waikato, New Zealand Maori Chiefs'
Artist unknown

The Rev. Samuel Leigh
Artist unknown

disposed to censure him; but when the committee met and realized it had only cost £35 for the passage of White and 'Shukey', and 'especially when they considered the strong temptation to which single men are exposed among savages', together with the 'painful situation' of Sister Turner, they agreed not to censure him but to allow him to return to New Zealand as a married man, taking with him also 'the young person' requested by Hobbs.[63]

White now embarked on a protracted hunt for a wife. But at the same time he did what he could for Hobbs, reporting on a visit to Margate, where he found 'Miss B' standing firm; and though her mother was likely to 'kick up a dust', having been to the mission house and 'made a good deal to do', he added that he hoped she would not stand out. ' "Trust in the Lord and he will provide". I long to be back again with you may God bless and make you a blessing, yours very affectionately Wm White.'[64]

It is possible that Miss Broggref's mother would have kicked up more dust if she could have read some of the missionaries' reports at this time. Turner wrote of the 'general *Apathy* and almost total Indifference' of the people around them: 'We have been amongst them upwards of three years but alas! as yet we have been tilling an unproductive soil. No real gospel spirit appears. No souls converted to God. . . . At times we feel much discouraged and our hands are ready to hang down. . . . The more we become acquainted with the People the more we see their dreadful depravity'.[65]

Hobbs's mood was summed up on his birthday: '1826 February 22nd. This day brings to a conclusion the twenty sixth year of my age. O my gracious creator for what purpose am I still in this howling wilderness with this frail and weakly body?'[66]

V: THE SACK OF WHANGAROA

In the year 1826 the barriers to communication seemed to be increasing and it was perhaps a mark of the frustration thus engendered that the year began and ended with a flogging. In January, a slave the Wesleyans had redeemed was caught stealing from the carpenter's shop, and they resolved to have him punished as an example. They sent for 'Taka'. his old master, to come and flog him. Towards evening he came, attended by other chiefs and people. Hobbs was away, but, with Stack, Turner talked to them for some time, explaining what end they had in view in proposing to punish the boy.

As Turner reported it, the assembled Maoris perfectly understood him and most appeared to approve. 'Taka', who had been to Port Jackson, explained how people were flogged for stealing there. He agreed to flog the boy, but as his hands were *tapu,* Turner tied the slave's hands 'and Taka gave him 15 or 16 stripes on his back with a stick, for which I gave him a hatchet. Our conduct we believe was generally approved, and we trust it will operate well among the children'.[1]

There is no evidence that it had this effect. The flogged boy was only a slave; there would have been instant uproar if such treatment was meted out to anyone else. The punishment may have seemed degrading or mean, but it can hardly have shocked children who heard of Hongi's wars. Stack described his boys' account of how the Bay of Islanders had met a Kaipara chief's wife with her four children aged four to nine. They got her to make a fire, then stuck her in the throat like a pig and drank her blood, then divided and cooked her body. Then they threw the children into the fire, throwing them back as they tried to escape. 'Our boys', wrote Stack, 'related this not only without feeling, but laughed heartily whilst mimicking the cries of the little ones.'[2]

Sometimes the missionaries felt they had achieved great things with the boys. On 5 February 1826, for example, they walked all the children in order to Te Puhi's village of Kaeo, 'and all being clean dressed', wrote Turner, 'they had a pretty appearance. Several of the people attended and listened attentively to what was said. We sang two Hymns with the children and then repeated a Prayer. Altogether we were pleased and encouraged with our Morning Service'.[3]

But these moments of encouragement were few; and in April Turner's eleven-month old baby died, after diarrhoea brought on, they thought, by teething troubles, despite a frantic hike by its father to the Bay of Islands for medicine. Hobbs made a coffin; the children were allowed to view the body and wept; the coffin was screwed down, they gave out a hymn and read the burial service of the Church of England. Then they walked down to the garden, buried the coffin, and walked in order home. In the evening there was prayer and Bible reading amid lightning and heavy showers. Shepherd of the CMS, who had waded breast high through flooded rivers, arrived to join them. Although the child's nurse cut herself in her grief, the funeral was almost a calculated contrast to the Maori *tangi*.[4]

This was the first death among the missionaries and it is possible it had greater significance among the Maoris than the missionaries realized, for it recurred frequently in discussons. But discussions were clearly on the decline during 1826. Sunday visits became almost entirely restricted to Te Puhi's village of Kaeo, Kearoa's village of Whaupuke, and to Pupuke and Toropapa, where in June they found their sacred rush house 'a den of thieves', after it had been damaged by the Bay of Islanders.[5] Few would listen and most of these in a critical spirit, not only raising theological objections but also questioning missionary attitudes and behaviour. The Maoris had enough experience of other kinds of Europeans to be able to compare the missionaries unfavourably, for example, with Pakeha-Maoris. There was no other European settlement in the area, but several runaway seamen passed through, receiving short shrift from the missionaries and relying instead on heathen charity. 'These men', wrote Turner, 'are becoming a great pest in the land.'[6]

In the Maori view, the missionaries were mean. 'On our observing that the reason we differed from the New Zealanders, was because of the goodness of God in bestowing upon us our Holy Religion Kia Roa asked us if it was God told us to demand seven baskets of potatoes for an axe. He said missionaries were a bad set, for they would not sell powder.' Just as the missionaries were horrified by cannibalism, so he was horrified by hanging, which he called murder. Jehovah was not a good God for commanding it, he said.[7] The boys at the school also thought that an English judge who condemned a man to be hung was a murderer.[8]

By the end of the year this continued resistance to their teaching had brought the missionaries to despair of success; 'the prophet', wrote Stack, in September, 'is called to prophesy to the dead bones, that they may live'.[9] But there was little sign of life. 'Oh! how low our prospects have long been with respect to the adult population', Stack wrote. 'They manifest total indifference and deadness to spiritual things. We often pass them near the Chapel and they are too lazy to accompany us a few yards to hear the word of life.'[10] When they held their monthly missionary prayer meeting they would read out of missionary journals, glorious gospel triumphs in Tahiti or in the Sandwich Islands and could only contrast them with 'This benighted corner of the earth'.[11]

Perhaps it was inevitable that as the teaching aspect of their task marked time they concentrated more on pioneering: people might not respond, but 'things' might be reduced to order. Here, as later in the Hokianga, they constantly bemoaned the pressure of secular activities but constantly found it difficult to break away.

Their farming flourished. In January they harvested enough wheat of excellent quality to keep them in bread till the ensuing harvest; and to encourage those Maoris who had begun to grow wheat they bought their crop, even though it had been seriously injured with 'the Red Gum'. For a week it was being brought in for sale and Turner supposed there had never been so much wheat bought and sold in New Zealand before.[12] In August, Stack recorded sowing more wheat;[13] in October Turner wrote that clearing, enclosing, and cultivating land was a cause of much anxiety, that the garden was well supplied with excellent vegetables. Most of this was Turner's work as the others knew little of agriculture and Stack was constitutionally unfit for it. Their cattle, a gift from Samuel Marsden, was now likely to increase very fast; they had eight including young calves. They were fencing in the wheat field and had moved the garden to another area because of flood damage. Because of all these activities they were not much out among the Maoris during the week.[14] Hobbs spent much of his time sawing and bringing in timber from the bush, or in carpentry around the mission or in fetching stores in the boat. During the year it became necessary to extend the mission premises. Mrs Wade, who arrived in the Bay of Islands in March, reached Whangaroa on 6 April[15] and Luke returned, after a twenty-month absence, with news of great interest in the mission in 'good Old England', on 28 October.[16] This, coupled with a revised plan of concentrating teaching activities on mission premises, led to a fresh outburst of building.

The building situation at the end of 1826 is shown in an undated drawing of Wesleydale by Nathaniel Turner, in possession of the Methodist Missionary Society, London (see Plate 1). The accompanying undated commentary by Turner states:

The long building at the back is a Rush House, 45 feet by 12—27 of which is a School Room, the remainder which is in two Rooms is occupied by Luke. The House below is our Dwelling. The main building of which is 26 by 13 with a skilling or Leanto at the back 10 feet wide and another at the southern end 8 feet. The Building to the right on the same level contains three apartments, two below and one above the one above serves as a Store for native Provisions etc etc. The skilling or Leanto is the Carpenters shop. The tall building above is the Barn and the small one to the right of it is the Cow House which is bush and log. The one down the Bank below is the Boat House, built of Rush. The Garden and young orchard are within the inner Fence below the House. The wheat Field is to the left of and below that. That below and to the left where the Cattle are seen Grazing is on Flat or uncultivated ground covered with small brush wood. The enclosures below are the native Plantations or kumara grounds. The River runs in the front and to the right and left in a very serpentine manner. The foreground is part of a native village. The principal village where the Pa is which could not be included is just to the left. The Hills immediately at the back are barren, but those in the distance are covered with fine Timber, Kaudi etc etc. The view of the settlement does not nearly equal the view in richness of scenery as from the Settlement.

That the scene described is in late 1826 can be established by the fact that the decision to build the rush house for use as a school is referred to on 3 October, the school commenced on 30 November, and Hobbs was still working on the school building on 9 December.[17] As a piece of pioneering, the mission station was an admirable achievement for so few men to have reached over a three-year period. But by now the work of evangelizing the heathen was reduced to its minimum; two hours a day from the one European incapable of heavy labour and a visit most Sundays to villages within a six-mile radius. It was not an onerous addition to the work all early settlers did, and in return they received continual financial support. In March, for example, a further seven tons of goods arrived for their use, at the same time as Mrs Wade;[18] and further articles of furniture arrived for their use from the Tonga mission.[19]

In July, Hobbs and Stack were, according to the rules, examined by Turner, as missionaries on trial; and their inadequacies were attributed to the secular needs of their situation. He reported that the result of the examination was not as favourable as he would wish. They now had Faith in Christ, though that of Stack was not strong, and were going on to Perfection though at too slow a rate. The instructions of the Committee, had, he believed, been generally observed and they had attended pretty regularly to private prayer. Their replies to questioning on evangelical repentance, he reported inadequate; they had read the Bible but all other

reading was of a desultory kind, especially in the case of
Hobbs; on the other hand they spent much time learning
Maori.[20] Hobbs was chastened by the examination and questioned afterwards in his journal whether he should be
considered as a missionary, though he might do as a
mechanic.[21]

During the year, disease contributed to social tension. At
the beginning of the year there was an epidemic, first found
among Maoris attached to the mission, then among the people
around. It was described as 'a sort of fever and thus of a
swelling of the head and face'. It did not affect the
Europeans.[22]

In December there was a widespread epidemic of influenza,
which appears to have spread from the Bay of Islands and
affected Europeans as well as Maoris. Turner's children were
feverish and 'almost choked with flegmatick obstruction of the
air passages'. On the 18th they received a visit from the Rev.
William Williams who administered medicine and bled some
of the mission Maoris, the first time this had been done at
Whangaroa. The epidemic did not cause many deaths; but it
was sufficiently severe and unusual to arouse a good deal of
fear. One of the mission boys told Stack they had had illness
at this time the previous year, now a worse one; perhaps the
next would kill them.[23]

At the same time as disease attacked them, so also did
neighbouring tribes. The first *taua* came from the Matauri
area. They came in March because of a *tapa,* or curse, a
woman of Ngatiuru had uttered against chief Tareha of the
Matauri area. One of his relatives had quarrelled with her
over some fruit; so in revenge she had called him *karaka,* or
fruit. On this occasion they appear merely to have attacked
some people in the bush.[24] In April, Ngatiuru planned to
attack Ngatipou, to have 'a potato fight' (or to rob them);
but frightened by the formidable appearance of their oppon-
ents they returned, after killing a few pigs.[25] This was followed
by reports of attack by Ngatipou.[26]

In May, Te Puhi's wife returned from Waimate, where
she had gone to cry over Hongi's son, killed at Kaipara, with

news that Hongi's wife had said that Te Puhi was a *kinaki,* or relish, for kumara. If Te Puhi had been equal in point of dignity with Hongi, Stack wrote, he would have gone and robbed him. Several places were likely to be attacked by Ngapuhi shortly and there was much anxiety whether Whangaroa was on the list.[27]

A few days later Hongi arrived, but in peace, on his way to Oruru to cry over a chief, 'Waidua', lately dead. He did not visit the missionaries, Stack wrote, because their signal for the sabbath was hoisted, and so they ate their 'English dinner' in peace. Afterwards they called on him on their way to the village and found him eating out of a basket of pipis, raised up so that he could eat them directly with his mouth, 'his hands being fastened behind him with the cords of superstition', Stack wrote. 'He could not but laugh with us at the folly of his proceeding. He bent forward his elbows for us to touch them instead of shaking hands.'[28]

In July there was news of the death of Pomare, a Bay of Islands chief and a rival of Hongi. He had gone to attack Ngatimaru, a tribe to the South, because they had joined Hongi in fighting the Kaipara people, Ngatiwhatua, who were related to Pomare. A *taua* of 170 went and only one returned to tell the tale.[29] Although Pomare's people had little to do with the Whangaroa people, it was all evidence of the declining power of northern tribes. For this reason they were increasingly reluctant to join Hongi in his wars,[30] even though this meant they continued to live under the threat of Hongi's attack. In October, for example, came a message from Hongi to Ngatiuru to leave their food and fly into the woods so that when he came he might not see their faces and kill them.[31]

Such troubles only seemed to beget further troubles. The standing menace of attack had a large part in the increasing disputes within Ngatiuru, disputes which in turn provoked further outside threats of attack. In June the missionaries were involved in conflict when Ngahuruhuru stole some boards from the saw-pit, which were recovered with the aid of two of the mission boys, Hika, his brother-in-law, and Hongi, son of Te Puhi. Stack noted much Maori discontent over the fact that the two youths had sided with the missionaries.[32] Ngahuruhuru was so enraged by Hika's conduct that he went home and vented his anger on his own children, who in turn went to Hika's parents, knocking their huts down and throwing their axes and pots into the river. Then he talked of going north to settle, later to visit the missionaries with a more formidable party than he could then raise.[33] Te Puhi, for his part, was having trouble with his wife, who was jealously claiming he had taken his brother George's widow as a wife.[34]

In September there was another quarrel, again originating with one of the younger chiefs. Young Te Puhi put a *rahui* on part of the woodland as a run for his pigs. Pepe, another chief, killed a pig of his which was grazing there, and sent portions of it to everyone, including young Te Puhi, who proceeded to pillage Pepe's residence. There was a general tumult, in which the older Te Puhi intervened and fought his brother Ngahuruhuru. He broke his sons' houses and put a *tapa,* or curse, on Ngahuruhuru and his pigs; and as a result they all expected to be robbed of their pigs by neighbouring tribes.[35]

The following month there was much more serious violence. One Sabbath Turner and Stack visited Te Puhi's rush chapel and, evidence enough of declining missionary influence, found only three women, the rest away digging fern-root; and going after them the missionaries found that Te Puhi had taken a long-handled hatchet and seriously injured a slave for setting the fern on fire to dig the roots more easily. The missionaries put a handkerchief round the man's head.

The slave had formerly belonged to He, principal wife of George, but now belonged to a man called Huna. The next day Huna and Mahue began to quarrel with Te Puhi over his treatment of the slave; his behaviour, they said, was *kino rawa,* very evil. Te Puhi took his musket, loaded it with two balls, and went towards the other two men. When he was six or eight yards away, Mahue put his spear in a position of defence expecting to be struck; but instead. Te Puhi shot him dead. Young Te Puhi, nephew of Mahue, took his musket in a passion, intending to shoot the old chief, but was restrained by his wife.

There was great uproar in the valley but the slave was killed, baked, and eaten as a sweet morsel; 'entombed in the bowels of our neighbours' as Stack put it, ghoulishly envisaging the two dead men as 'naked spirits before the awful tribunal of a Righteous God', lifting up their eyes in 'the gloomy mansions of the damned'.[36]

The death of Mahue was yet another reason to expect attack. In November there were rumours that Titore, the Bay of Islands chief, was coming to avenge the murder.[37] Turner reported the people in a state of consternation and dread from a report of a party coming and that they had abandoned their *pa* and lived in temporary sheds on a hill at the back of the mission station which was a good lookout point.[38] Te Puhi talked of going north and said that the Bay of Islanders would be taking over the area and becoming the missionaries' people.[39]

Shortly a *taua* of two to three hundred people came, killed and ate a 'fine young woman' who was a slave of Te Puhi's, leaving her bones on the beach beneath the *pa* to be gnawed by the pigs. Te Puhi himself skulked in the bush with three loaded muskets. Undisturbed, the *taua*—'such a set of determined villians I never before saw'—set to work and plundered young kumara, corn, taro, and potato, destroying the labour of weeks in a few minutes. They also attacked the mission station, trampling down wheat, destroying fences, stealing potatoes and onions, the mission canoe and two oars, and chopping two wheelbarrows to pieces for the iron. In a scuffle, Hobbs lost his hat: doubtless it was a tempting trophy. Believing the attackers capable of anything, the missionaries tied up their journals and private papers in readiness for flight. But the *taua* left, taking with them two slaves.

Later the missionaries learnt that the party came from the coast between Whangaroa and the Bay of Islands and that although the pretext was to avenge the death of Mahue, the seasonal shortage of potatoes was the main reason for the attack.[40] One result of the episode was that the missionaries set the mission Maoris to cutting back the undergrowth on the way to a hill five miles south, from whence a horse and cart could take them to Kerikeri.[41] Clearly they were planning an escape route.

The Wesleyans were not alone in experiencing disorders. Henry Williams, in early December, reported trouble at CMS mission stations of Rangihoua and Kerikeri, and at Paihia it was an uncertain peace. The Maoris, he thought, were in a singular state of mind, very unsettled.[42] As James Kemp reported it, two chiefs and many others from the Bay of Islands had been cut off in the Waikato. Hongi, in October, had been taken with a violent pain in his knee and had to be carried about. One of his daughters had recently died of consumption; his blind wife Turi, who had been a leading spirit in his campaigns, was dying, painfully, of the same disease. Then, one of his other wives, of whom he was very fond, was seduced by his son-in-law. The man shot himself and the wife hanged herself.

There were various explanations of the troubles besetting Hongi. One was that he was bewitched by Maoris 'up towards the eastward' to prevent him from attacking them. Others blamed the missionary god, especially where disease was concerned. But various other developments were making the missionaries especially unpopular. The CMS were talking of opening a station further inland, which was unpopular in the Bay. The expedition of the first New Zealand Company, under Captain James Herd, had arrived and many Maoris were elated at the prospect of settlers who would be a better source of muskets than missionaries and less uncomfortable neighbours. The CMS were beset with rumours that they might be sent away to make room for the Company settlers; or that if Hongi died, they would be plundered. But Hongi, in any case, was planning to move to Whangaroa.[43]

At Whangaroa itself, the sense of foreboding grew. At the beginning of December, when the sky threatened thunder that never came and Stack thought that disease must be in the atmosphere, rumours of Hongi kept going round. 'The native mind at present', wrote Stack, 'is certainly in great agitation and prospects with us wear a black appearance.' People took to living at the *pa* for refuge; Te Puhi fixed one of the carronades from the *Boyd* at the top of the *pa,* though he had no idea how to fire it. Quarrels continued. Hongi, Te Puhi's son, fired at a target, naming it after one of the chiefs; 'the natives say it is a tapa', wrote Stack, 'and likely to create broils with us and the natives'.[44]

The missionary situation was becoming increasingly difficult. George, who had, in his way, protected them, was dead; Te Puhi and Ngahuruhuru, even if they had the will, probably no longer had the authority. In so far as the missionaries had undermined the local leadership, their dilemma was to that extent the harvest they had sown. Their policy of excluding people from parts of the mission premises continued. In November Te Puhi attempted to enter Hobbs's shop, was forced out and in a rage asked whose place it was that they pushed him out? Hobbs in reply asked him who had bought the land?[45] A few days later, when the *taua* was about to attack, he asked the missionaries how many muskets they had and they in turn asked what he thought muskets could do for them? 'What said he would you allow your premises to be quietly broken up and make no resistance?'[46] Others began to ask them what they would do when Ngatiuru left and other tribes attacked the mission station?[47] In retrospect, these were to seem highly significant questions.

One index of the rising tension was the increasing difficulty in coping with the children, especially those of the local chiefs. When Turner put a child of Te Puhi's out of the yard the boy threw a heavy piece of hard clay, which hurt Turner's arm considerably. 'This boy', he wrote angrily, 'though not more perhaps than 8 years old, I durst not chastise for fear of bringing myself into trouble. Nor yet will his parents for fear, either as they say, that the Boy would go and hang himself or that others hearing what the Parents had done would come and chastise and rob them for such conduct. Such is the state of New Zealand.'[48]

The next trouble came from the son of the late chief George, aged about twelve to thirteen, who had begun to steal from the mission. Turner reckoned that he had taken at least twelve to fifteen fowls, and he was now starting on the ripening wheat. After a while, the missionaries decided

to try and stop the thefts by catching the boy and giving
him a 'good beating'. They mentioned their plan to the
chiefs, and were under the impression that Te Puhi in particular approved of their intention. On 20 December the
boy stole more of their wheat while they were at prayers in
company with the Reverend William Williams, who was
visiting them. They were unable to find the boy, but a few
hours later his mother brought him to their yard. Turner
wrote: 'We went out to her and enquired what she wanted,
to which she replied to have her son whipped. Mr Hobbs
immediately fetched a vine stick and while he was so doing
Mr Williams and I spoke to her, and asked if it was right for
Him to come and steal so many of our things to which she
replied as before "What are your things that they should not
be stolen?" Mr Hobbs gave him two sharp strokes and with
those he got away'.[49]

The mother immediately ran towards the village, making a
great noise, and within ten minutes all the people of the
valley surrounded the mission house quite naked and in a
great rage, as was Te Puhi when he arrived, a musket in
each hand. 'We told him not to be hasty', wrote Hobbs, 'but
to stop and let us have an understanding. He said it was not
proper to beat a gentleman though it might be to beat a
slave. We then reminded him of having said it would be very
good to flog the lad if he continued his thefts and asked
what we were to do? He said we must not flog a rangatira.'[50]

Old Te Puhi and Ngahuruhuru pacified the people, and
although there were a few minor thefts, they all returned
home after a while. 'This is one of the most serious frays
we have had', wrote Turner, 'but we are not without hope
that it will turn out to good account at last.'[51]

The following day there was more uproar when Stack
attempted to put a young man out of the yard. He was
struck three blows from a 'native weapon called a Harojo'
and Te Puhi again attempted, not very successfully, to
mediate on the missionaries behalf. The next day, Stack
left with Williams for Kerikeri where he learnt 'we are not
alone in the trials of the desert' since there was Maori unrest
there also. The next few days were spent at Paihia, much in

the company of the CMS farmer Richard Davis, but more especially with his daughter Mary Ann. At prayer meetings he felt himself 'carried back to civilized life'; on Christmas Day he went with William Williams to Waitangi where they spoke to a party including the brother of Christian Rangi (who had been baptized by the CMS on the eve of his death). 'They seemed much disposed to cavil', wrote Stack, 'and said they had been praying a long time to Jehovah for his Spirit but had not yet received it. They said Christian Ranghi had returned from the invisible world and that he was not gone to Heaven but to the Reinga.'[52]

On 30 December Stack arrived back at Wesleydale with Davis and his daughter.[53] The last day of the year 1826 was, for Turner, 'a profitable day to my own soul'[54] and Hobbs recorded that 'The Lord was gracious to us while we passed the old year out and the new year in. . . .'[55] At the same time, Stack wrote that there were only two or three natives when they held service at Te Puhi's place.

In Turner's view, 'things wear but a gloomy aspect'. He noted the succession of murders and suicides that had lately occurred in Hongi's family and that Hongi had left Waimate and was now on his way to take possession of Whangaroa, or some part of it, as his future residence. 'Whether he intends killing or driving away the present inhabitants, or what may be his design, is unknown. We see ourselves in a precarious situation.'[56] Distracted by all these problems, Turner's existence was complicated by the birth of another son on 3 December.[57]

As the new year came in, George Clarke of the CMS at Kerikeri was still writing of alarms and quarrels among the Maoris. 'A general disapprobation of Hongi's proceedings is very evident, and I think there is a storm brewing which for a time may affect the Mission. Various reports are brought to us; they principally amount to this, that it is Hongi's intention to plunder us and send us away: we are unwilling to believe such statements.'[58] The same day at Whangaroa, Hobbs wrote that the year had begun with some uncertainty and anxiety for them. Two days earlier Hongi had entered the heads of Whangaroa Harbour with 400 men but his future intentions were uncertain. He was, wrote Hobbs, 'like the troubled sea which cannot rest whose waters cast up mire and dirt'.[59]

The first news of this long-expected arrival had come on the evening of 4 January. Hobbs and Stack were 'engaged in Native devotion with our domesticks' when Hika's father came, almost out of breath, calling for his son to flee with him, as Hongi had entered the harbour and already killed some of Ngatipou. Later Te Puhi came to collect his gunpowder, which had been stored at the mission, and confirmed the report; now what use would the missionaries' *karakia* be to them? he asked. If they had plenty of muskets it would be well. As he left to go home in the dark, one of the mission boys spoke of danger from the *atua;* but it was clear that Te Puhi was now more afraid of Hongi than the supernatural.[60]

The next day, amid general lamentation, Te Puhi, Ngahuruhuru and others left the valley for the Hokianga, after taking, according to Stack, an affectionate leave of the missionaries. However, many remained, including wives and children. Amid conflicting reports of whether they were to be attacked or not, the missionaries spent Friday and Saturday harvesting their wheat.[61]

On Sunday the 7th a woman from Hongi's family arrived with a message.[62] He was still down at the heads, besieging Ngatipou in their *pa* at Pinia, and a battle was expected the following day. Ngatiuru, especially those with a grievance against Ngatipou, were invited to join him. He had not intended attacking Ngatiuru and was angry that Te Puhi had fled. The next day, at the flowing of the tide, everyone in the valley left in their canoes to join Hongi, partly because they wanted to join in, partly because they feared that once Hongi had attacked Ngatipou, they themselves would be attacked by Ngatipou's powerful allies, Te Rarawa. The missionaries were told that they themselves would be robbed and perhaps killed by Te Rarawa; also that a party was coming from Hokianga to take them away. In the morning some Bay of Islanders leapt over the fence and stole a pot, cocking a musket at Luke Wade when he tried to restrain them. By Monday evening, all was silent in the valley, save for the barking of the dogs forsaken by their masters. 'We are entirely left to shift for ourselves', wrote Stack.[63]

Although there was no disturbance through the night, it was clear that the missionaries could expect to be plundered, either by Te Rarawa or by marauding parties associated with the conflict. They conferred after breakfast on the Tuesday and decided that Stack, accompanied by Tawena, a redeemed slave, the only one who had not left them, should go to Kerikeri for help and advice. At noon, Puru, another redeemed slave, arrived from the Bay of Islands with news that the brig *Wellington,* which had been taken by rebels, had been recaptured by the joint effort of missionaries and ships' captains.[64]

About the same time as Puru arrived, twelve Ngapuhi also came, led by the son of the late Pomare of Kororareka Bay. 'We enquired what they were come for', wrote Turner, 'to which they replied "to take away your things and burn down your house, for your place is deserted and you are broken".' Pomare's son was invited in and given food; more food was passed out to the rest of the band outside. Despite this they began to steal pigs and tried to break into Luke Wade's house. As it happened they were known by Mary Ann Davis, who was still staying at the mission, and they treated her with respect and brought back stolen goods at her request. They then went to dig kumara; but on their return they broke into the potato house, demanded paper for cartridges and attempted to steal the mission's new boat but then decided against it. Tawena heard them saying it would not do to plunder the missionaries as they were too few to take all the blame—better to join in a larger party. He advised the missionaries to hide things as they would be robbed the next day.[65]

During the day they also learnt that Ngatipou had fled from their *pa* and that Ngapuhi were in pursuit of them; that Hongi now intended to return to Waimate and that the Whangaroa people were going to accompany him. If so, wrote Turner, the mission could not continue.[66]

At 10 p.m. Stack left for Kerikeri. He was accompanied by

The Rev. Nathaniel Turner
Engraving by J. Cochran

John Hobbs. Miniature painted
by Major Sturgeon at Hokianga in 1830

Tawena who carried all their journals, together with a small parcel for Mrs Turner in his pack; a heavy burden so that Stack had to keep stopping for him. Nonetheless, the moon shone perfectly and the missionaries' recent improvements to the track enabled them to travel more easily. At Kerikeri they were hospitably received when they arrived wet and cold as the morning star rose in the sky; and at once a messenger left for Marsden's Vale (Paihia) with Turner's note.[67]

Back at Whangaroa, as the missionaries prepared for bed, two of the mission girls returned with more news of what was happening at the heads. They confirmed that Ngatipou had left the *pa* and that Hongi was in pursuit. When the *pa* was entered only two old ladies remained, one the mother of Te Pere. Both were murdered and a slave girl killed, 'cut up like a pig, roasted and eaten'. They could tell nothing encouraging of missionary prospects; there had been talk of robbing them, but whether this would happen or not, they could not tell. Finally at midnight the missionaries retired to rest; if not free of anxiety, wrote Turner, free of disturbing fear.[68]

Soon after daybreak on 10 January 1827 Turner was awakened by Luke Wade, with the news that a party was approaching the house. He dressed and went out. Hobbs was already out and asking two of the leading men why they had come? 'They said in broken English to make a fight I then asked, why were they thus coming? to which they replied your chief has fled and every person has left the place and you will be completely striped before noon and therefore go. To this I said Where must we go? Go into the woods said they be off.'[69] At this the plundering began. Within fifteen minutes Luke Wade's house, the potato house, the outer kitchen, and the upper store had been broken open and the contents carried off; then similarly the carpenter's shop was attacked. Several guns were fired, 'after which the number of natives greatly increased', wrote Hobbs, 'and amongst them were some of our own People'.[70]

However, at this moment, four of the mission boys came back and offered to help. They agreed to help the missionaries in the twenty-mile flight to Kerikeri. They put on some of the missionaries' clothes, to be returned at the end of the journey. While the children were prepared, the girls made the inevitable pot of tea, and a bag full of 'victuals' was collected; but then, as windows began to be broken and marauders began coming through the back door, they left through the front door, going down the garden for the last time, through the fence and over the wheat field. 'I could not but praise the Lord almost every step I took from the premises', wrote Turner, 'for I viewed myself and companions like Lot of old fleeing from the City of Destruction.'[71]

As well as their Maori helpers, the party included the Turners, their three children, the youngest an infant five weeks old, Mr and Mrs Luke Wade, Hobbs, and Miss Davis. They carried with them only a small trunk containing changes for the children and a few bundles in their hands. They had abandoned property Turner reckoned was to the value of £1,500-£2,000, and he wrote that he felt the force of the words: 'Skin for skin yea all that a Man hath will he give for his life.'[72]

It was a foggy morning and in the heavy dew the 'poor women' became quite wet passing through the corn field. They made their way through the kumara grounds, 'no longer sacred to any parties', and over the river.[73] Here they met some of Ngatiuru who had fled to Hokianga the previous Friday. One of them was the man who had nearly killed Turner the day before the *Mercury* had been taken; another had been involved in killing the crew of the *Boyd*. From these they learned that Te Puhi was coming with a powerful *taua* of a thousand men from Hokianga, to defend the place from Ngapuhi; that they would strip the missionaries of all they had and murder them if they did not hide in the bush.

For a while they did so; but eventually Turner persuaded them to go forward.[74] As they did so, they met Ngahuruhuru and a Bay of Islands chief, Te Wharenui, whose wife was a sister of the Hokianga chiefs, Nene and Patuone.[75] These advised them to stop but agreed to accompany them for protection. Soon they met a war party of two to three hundred men, half of them armed with muskets, the rest with bayonets or long-handled hatchets. 'This was a solemn moment', wrote Hobbs, 'and God our heavenly father no doubt looked upon us as his defenceless servants with peculiar care.'[76] The party was led by Patuone, who clearly had great authority and who came forward to rub noses and show his friendship and goodwill. Te Puhi also appeared, 'evidently labouring under inward emotions of a very distressing kind', wrote Hobbs.[77] After a consultation among the chiefs, the missionaries were told to go on one side.[78] The fighting men were ordered to proceed as fast as possible to the mission station and the missionaries were allowed to proceed, although, Hobbs added, several wished them to remain there, 'for what reason I cannot say'. Te Wharenui and Ngahuruhuru accompanied them for protection. They made their way through the woods, where they were met by Stack and Clarke with eight or ten CMS mission Maoris, one of whom was sent back to fetch chairs to carry the women. At the waterfall six miles from Kerikeri they were met by a strong party from Paihia, including Henry Williams, Richard Davis, and William Puckey, with at least a dozen Maoris.[79]

At Kerikeri, Stack, who had walked nearly fifty miles since ten the previous evening, retired to bed; Turner and Hobbs discussed their predicament with their CMS colleagues. Kemp told them that both Te Wharenui and Titore had said they must not remain at Kerikeri because they were liable to be murdered as refugees. It was decided they must go on to Marsden's Vale the next day, where they would have the protection of the shipping. It was also decided that Turner and his family should go to Port Jackson.

The next day, before the missionaries left for Marsden's Vale, the Maoris who had helped them were rewarded with slop clothing out of the mission stores, only to be robbed immediately by Titore's slaves, because they were refugees.[80] At Marsden's Vale, which they reached at noon, Stack and Hobbs stayed with Davis, Luke Wade and his wife with Fairburn, and the Turners with Henry Williams. Turner went on board the *Sisters* (Captain Duke) and arranged a passage to New South Wales for his family. At this stage it was thought Hobbs and Stack would remain.[81]

That evening they had a message from Kerikeri that Hongi,

in pursuit of Ngatipou, had been wounded perhaps mortally; and chief Rewa had warned them that if he died, Kerikeri station would also be plundered.[82] The next day the most valuable possessions were removed from Kerikeri but most of the CMS remained at their post. There were frequent rumours of Hongi's death, but on the 16th news came that he was alive and that Kerikeri was in no immediate danger.[83]

The danger was receding, but Turner persisted in his intention of returning to New South Wales. By now he had booked a passage also for the Wades and a 'native' girl and boy, taken as servants because 'we cannot do without some person as a servant'. Although Turner thought Hobbs should remain because they had heard that White was coming from England with Hobbs's intended wife, he felt that Stack should also return. Stack, however, wished to stay; presumably because of Miss Davis. Turner justified their departure on the grounds that all advised it was impracticable to start another mission at the moment and they lacked the resources. Also, their bodies were 'completely unnerved' by recent events.[84] On the other hand, Henry Williams was not convinced they needed to return to the Colony. 'Their relinquishing the mission altogether, according to their present views, does not meet our approbation, as they have a place of refuge: but this is for their consideration.'[85]

News continued to come in about Hongi. His principal wife, Turi, had died and was buried at 'Ahauroro', the place where the *Mercury* had been plundered. Later her bones would be brought back to Waimate.[86] Hongi was now beseiging the *pa* of the chief Matapo, of the tribe Kai Tangata (men eaters). The women and children of Ngatipou had been horribly murdered. Tinana was said to have butchered nearly a hundred women and children himself.[87] Later there was news of the destruction of Kai Tangata, Matapo's people. Men, women, and children were slaughtered, and mangled bodies littered the ground, or were carried about in baskets to be devoured. 'A number of bodies were spread before Hongi to appease and cheer him in his dark afflictive hour and as a sort of satisfaction or rather revenge for having been wounded.'[88] But in the Waikato, news had it, Ngatimaru were so overjoyed at the news of Hongi's wound, they did little else but 'dance both day and night'.[89]

On the 19 January, a meeting was held with the CMS and it was finally decided that Hobbs and Stack should also go back to New South Wales. There seem to have been three reasons for this. The first was a rumour of a possible attack on Marsden's Vale.[90] The second was that if the CMS also had to flee, the *Herald* might soon be the only ship in the bay and there would not be enough room in it, especially with the prospect of storms.[91] The final reason was that a letter had been received from Captain James Herd of the first New Zealand Company's ship, the *Rosanna,* that the Hokianga people had planned to attack Wesleydale before leaving home. Hitherto there had been an idea that the Wesleyans might start another mission under the auspices of Patuone: now this looked less promising. On the 20th, Stack and Hobbs booked passage for the Colony on the *Sisters.*[92] On the 22nd, Hika arrived from the Hokianga, and pleaded to accompany Hobbs to New South Wales.[93]

Prospects looked dangerous whether they stayed or left. Rumours continued of a possible attack on Paihia by the Kawakawa people; and on the 23rd, Stack wrote of helping the CMS bury some of their iron goods secretly by night.[94] But the voyage on the *Sisters* looked equally risky; their fellow passengers were the mutineers of the *Wellington,* being taken back to the Colony in irons for punishment. On the 24th it was discovered they had cut their irons in readiness for revolt when out of the Bay. That evening, as one of the whalers hoisted her colours and the ships alternately fired a gun, Stack supposed that corporal punishment was being inflicted on the prisoners.[95]

On Saturday 27th with the prisoners all secured once more, they were ready to sail. They assembled at five at Henry Williams's place, to pray for safety on the deep and for the CMS left among 'the unfeeling cannibals of New Zealand', as Stack put it.[96] They went on board, accompanied by Williams, Davis, Fairburn, and Puckey; and next day, escorted by the brig *Wellington,* they sailed. 'We left a large party at Korerarika Bay under the direction of Taria', wrote

Hobbs. 'The Church mission Brethren felt very anxious about him when we left and we could not but feel much for our dear friends who were remaining behind amongst such unprincipled savages.'[97]

During the voyage the missionaries tried to influence the prisoners; but they proved indifferent. Many were Roman Catholics and would not read the tracts distributed among them. On 3 February a plot was discovered, whereby the prisoners hoped, with the aid of two seamen, to murder the captain and officers and carry the ship away to South America. The Captain had their hands manacled behind their backs. On Friday 9 February they anchored in Sydney Cove and, going ashore, met their brethren Mansfield and Horton.[98] The first phase of the mission had ended.

PART TWO

VI: WHY WAS WHANGAROA ATTACKED?

It is easy to describe the attack on Whangaroa; but motives are less explicable. The argument over what had happened developed soon after the missionaries' arrival in Sydney. Their initial welcome from their colleagues Mansfield and Horton was 'most hearty and consolitary',[1] and the following Sunday when Turner told his story to a crowded congregation in Macquarie Street Chapel 'for two hours the auditory were in tears, and petrified with horror'. Reporting this, the *Sydney Gazette* expressed its satisfaction that Hongi, 'this savage monster', responsible for the sack of Whangaroa, was wounded and unlikely to survive.[2]

On 15 February, a special District Meeting was held in Sydney at which Turner, Hobbs, and Stack were joined by their colleagues Mansfield, Horton, and Weiss. Having heard an account of the abandonment of Whangaroa, the meeting decided unanimously that the Brethren had acted with the utmost prudence and firmness and that they were justified in relinquishing their station and proceeding to the colony. Rather surprisingly, the meeting concurred in Turner's view that he had no capacity for the Maori language, that he should 'cultivate his talent for English preaching' and that he should be stationed for the moment in Samuel Leigh's circuit, at Parramatta. Hobbs and Stack were to continue the study of Maori; Weiss was received on trial for work in Tonga, though his departure was to be delayed until the arrival of White, who was to be chairman of the South Sea Islands district.[3]

The missionaries also printed their own account of recent happenings, which was first printed in Sydney and subsequently reprinted in missionary journals.[4] Marsden, returning in April after a New Zealand visit, loyally confirmed that their account contained nothing but matters of fact, that the picture was not too highly coloured nor the truth in any way distorted.[5]

Such protestations are a hint that there were criticisms to answer. Years later, Hobbs was to complain of an unkind reception from his colleagues in New South Wales, who treated them, he thought, 'rather as refugees or runaway missionaries who had unduly deserted their post than as sufferers in the cause'.[6] Entries in Hobbs's journal at this time also indicate strain in relations with them.[7]

It is probable that as the months passed and it was clear the CMS were still at their posts, having survived the apparent perils, men began to wonder whether it had been truly necessary for the Wesleyans to leave. In August, when the *Sydney Gazette* learnt the Wesleyans planned to return to New Zealand, that unpromising 'emporium of cannibalism', it argued that as the CMS were already established there, the Wesleyans should concentrate instead on the Friendly Islands.[8]

Such were the controversies at the time; and argument has continued ever since. The pro-missionary version sees them as heroic victims of circumstances beyond their control—in Strachan's oft-quoted words, it had been 'one of the most noble, best sustained, and protracted struggles, to graft Christianity upon a nation, savage and ferocious, which the history of the Church of Christ supplies'.[9] Alfred Saunders, on the other hand, thought their reasons for abandoning their work were not satisfactory; such people as 'the timid Mrs Turner and the delicate Mr Leigh' lacked the necessary 'vigorous health, courage and determination'; and he thought that the return of Stack and Hobbs to New Zealand showed the survival of the fittest.[10]

Perhaps with the passage of time a compromise between such extreme interpretations will emerge; but there are two problems in the ending of the Whangaroa mission which can now be reconsidered. These are Hongi—his attitude to the missionaries and his motives for attacking Whangaroa; and the role and motives of the Whangaroa people in the crisis.

One of the few missionaries who attempted to analyse why Hongi attacked the people of Whangaroa was George Clarke, of the CMS. He reported various Maori explanations: that it was a satisfaction for the death of his wife who had hanged herself; that it was a satisfaction for the murder of crew and passengers of the *Boyd* and for the plunder of the *Mercury*. But in his view all such reasons were subterfuges; Whangaroa had great advantages in the procuring of muskets and powder and this was what moved Hongi. If he lived at Whangaroa, ships would anchor there for refreshment and he could supply them with an abundance of local timber.[11]

Much depends on our guess at what manner of man Hongi was. Perhaps behind the ebb and flow of rumour and counter rumour of what he was planning, there was a cool, calculating mind pursuing rational objectives; and perhaps for much of his life Hongi was such a man. But it would be hard, even for a calculating man, to maintain his balance amid the troubles that beset him at the end of 1826: campaigns to the south going wrong, opposition in the Bay of Islands building up; successive children dying or killed; one wife killing herself after an affair with another man; and his blind wife, Turi, who had guided him on so many of his campaigns, now in the last stages of consumption. George Clarke at this time thought that in a few years 'neither root nor branch of that once flourishing family' would be left;[12] and most thought that, if it was not the missionary God afflicting him, then Hongi was bewitched.[13]

Whatever the possibility of rational objectives, there is the look of a man defying fate, even perhaps courting disaster, in the story of Hongi's last months; and as for his attitude to the Wesleyans, there is again, a choice of explanations. Hobbs was told by King and Shepherd, that while at Rangihoua, Hongi had talked of plundering the Wesleyans.[14] There is evidence that he was indifferent to their fate: 'Some say that Shonghi laughed when he heard what had befallen us', wrote Stack.[15] Finally there was William Williams's evidence. Hongi told him he had intended to have the missionaries living with him; that while he was pursuing the enemy, the mission station was plundered, without his knowledge and contrary to his wish, by parties which had accompanied him from the Bay of Islands; and Williams believed this was the truth.[16]

There is no evidence that Hongi himself plundered the mission; he was busily pursuing the enemy and being wounded. But his followers were involved, and he shared in the benefits: Stack at Rangihoua heard that 'Tariha danced in six blankets before Ware Porka and asked him if he would not go and look for some; and that Shonghi's wife is dead and was buried in 4 of our blankets'.[17]

If Hongi's motives are hard to unravel, even more so are those of Ngatiuru. The problem here is to decide their attitude to the mission. Were they agreed in their attitude, or were they divided? Did they try to protect the mission, did they join in the plundering, or did they even instigate the plundering; and if they plundered, why? Not all these questions can be finally answered, but certainly they were involved in the plundering.

Turner, unlike his two colleagues, attempted to disguise this fact. In describing how the remaining Ngatiuru left to join Hongi's party, he wrote that they left in perfect goodwill, concerned at parting; the school children were forced to go along by their parents and guardians, 'though very much against the will of some of them'.[18] Again, in his description of the attack, he made no reference to any Ngatiuru among the plunderers. Finally, in the official account printed after arrival in Sydney, the attackers were identified only as a strange tribe: 'We demanded their business. They said, "We are come to make a fight." "But why do you wish to do this?" we asked. They replied, "Your chief has fled, and all your people have left the place, and you will be stripped of all your property before noon; therefore, instantly be gone." Oro, the chief who made this declaration, and whose residence is at Wyemattee [Te Waimate], gave orders in the same moment to the rest to break open a small house that was occupied by Luke Wade'.[19]

This version has strongly influenced subsequent accounts: Findlay and Holdsworth, for example, had a 'detachment of

Hongi's men' being marched up to the mission house, under a commander who gave the order to attack, as if they were disciplined Redcoats.[20]

It is not untrue that the attack was begun by members of Hongi's following; but this is only part of the story. Hobbs wrote in his journal: 'This business had not been commenced long before a gun or two was fired after which the number of the natives greatly increased and amongst them were some of our own People.' At the same time, some of the former mission boys also came up: he distinguished between the two.[21]

It is true that Hobbs did not actually refer to Ngatiuru plundering the mission station; but it is unlikely that they refrained from joining in. The missionaries had in fact expected to be plundered by their own tribe before the last of them left to join Hongi. 'As we are not certain but the few natives who are going down with the tide after midnight may not try to rob us we have agreed that each Brother take his turn for a portion of the night in watching', wrote Stack.[22] Later Stack was to write in the margin of a report home: '. . . Ngate Huru the tribe amongst whom we laboured formed part of the plunderers of our Mission Station; even Te Puhi's wife was one of the most active. And from our domestics we learn that in butchering the unhappy creatures left in the Pa of Ngate Po they signalized themselves for atrocity.'[23]

William Williams of the CMS put it more strongly. 'It appears I think beyond a doubt', he wrote, 'though our Wesleyan friends are loathe to believe it, that their own chief, Tepui, was the instigator of the whole business. The people who broke into the house said that they were desired to do so by Tepui's wife and Hongi himself confirmed the same report: but the strongest proof is that Tepui at the head of a large body of Hukeanga natives whom he collected for the purpose, carried away the greatest part of the plunder.'[24] Later, on a visit to Hongi, Williams wrote: 'It was . . . painful to witness the indifference with which the Whangaroa natives living with Hongi regard all that has passed.'[25] George Clarke wrote a similar version, emphasizing Hongi's innocence, and stating specifically that the ringleader of the plunderers was Te Puhi's wife, acting on her husband's orders.[26]

There are other clues which offer support to this theory. Stack, for example, was puzzled by the fact that when Te Puhi and Ngahuruhuru fled for the Hokianga, wives and children (presumably including Te Puhi's head wife) remained. Some of those who remained, he wrote, claimed to be related to the Bay of Islanders.[27] Te Puhi's wife was apparently closely related to Hongi; as has been mentioned, she had gone to Waimate in May to cry over Hongi's son killed at Kaipara; and from her had come much of the news of Hongi's attitude and intentions.[28]

One final clue as to the role of Te Puhi's wife is in Hobbs's description of his first meeting with Te Puhi and his 'worthless wife' when he returned to Hokianga. To Hobbs, the old man appeared 'quite hardened and more like a swine than a man'; they told him they could no longer treat him as they did when he was the chief at Whangaroa. 'He was very disobliging, and careless of our feelings; and his wife retains all her former impudence and was quite annoying. I told Te Puhi I was not ill-affected towards him but wished him not to bring his wife about the premises. He wished to know why we did not like his wife, and in answer we told him that her whole conduct at Whangaroa was most displeasing to us; and that we wished as things were now so altered not to have anything to do with her. Such a woman I think I never saw'.[29]

The passage suggests there was a great deal in relationships at Whangaroa which was never recorded in letters and journals; it is a hint also that, contrary to Clarke's theory which blamed Te Puhi for the attack, the Wesleyans may have come to attribute more blame to his wife.

Te Puhi's flight to the Hokianga, and his return with a war-party, presents similar difficulties of interpretation. It is clear the missionaries did not suspect Te Puhi at the time of the attack. Not only did they think they had parted in friendship; when they met him during their flight to Kerikeri, Turner referred to him as 'our poor old chief Te Puhi'; and Hobbs thought him 'labouring under inward emotions of a very distressing kind'. Perhaps the emotion was fear he would arrive at Wesleydale too late for loot. William Williams later heard that Te Puhi on this occasion wanted to strip Turner and the missionaries but was prevented by Patuone.[30] On 19 January, Henry Williams was recorded as hearing from Captain Herd, of the New Zealand Company's ship *Rosanna,* then in the Hokianga, not only that the Hokianga people had a great deal of Whangaroa mission property, but also that before leaving they had said they were going to rob the missionaries.[31] It is true that old Captain Herd was not the most reliable of witnesses of Maori thought and action; it is true also that many threats to attack mission stations were being made at this time and not carried out; on the other hand, since the mission station had been deserted by its tribe, it could be expected that all neighbouring tribes would hold that according to the practice of *muru* it was open to plunder.

Yet another report came from Hobbs's boy Hika, after a visit to Hokianga. He said that the Hokianga people came intending plunder, but only after persuasion by a chief named Hauhau. 'Tepui opposed the proposition as did also *Patuone* (the popular chief) the latter however pleaded as the greatest reason that he was among the party and would share in the odium which the white people would cast upon all concerned in it, but if he were not amongst them he would readily consent. However the eloquence of Hauhau prevailed over regard for character and every other consideration and several miles distant from Wesleydale before they had any apprisal of what the Bay of Islanders had begun they came to a fixed determination to rob the missionaries'.[32]

It is possible to suspect that Hika was attempting to defend the good name of Te Puhi; and it is evident that the missionaries were still very dependent on the mission boys for news of what was happening. In the last few days at Whangaroa Stack had recorded Hika as saying that a party would be coming to take them to live in the Hokianga, adding, 'But he merely seemed to be speaking jestingly'; and he recorded his gratitude that 'Tawenga', a slave, was staying with them, as he would be useful as an interpreter or to warn them of any serious intention among strangers.[33]

Missionary ignorance of what was happening around them, is, therefore, a major handicap, particularly in attempting to reconstruct motives. There is enough evidence to suggest that Ngatiuru participated in plundering the mission station; and some indication that they may have instigated it. Such evidence is persistent in the case of Te Puhi's wife. But why should they have wanted to plunder the missionaries? There are many possible explanations, but two are particularly plausible.

The first is that they genuinely fled for fear of Hongi; in any case, successive plunderings had made the threat of starvation very real if they stayed. But once they left, the missionaries were a people without a tribe and could be expected to be plundered by the first party that could attack them. Since this was now inevitable, Ngatiuru might as well be among the first to enjoy the loot, particularly as this would endear them to their Hokianga protectors. They may also have thought of buying off Hongi's threats by creating a situation where he could share in the looting.

But there are some difficulties in this explanation. One is that part of Ngatiuru stayed and joined Hongi and to this extent it can be questioned whether they were afraid of him. It is also possible that their Hokianga allies were coming to protect Ngatiuru in possession of their lands.

The alternative explanation is that Ngatiuru wished from the beginning to plunder the missionaries. They could not simply do this themselves; this would invite European retribution, something which even Hongi and Patuone were anxious to avoid. But if a situation could be created in which it was impossible to attach the blame to any one group, then it would become a possibility; and in the event, no retribution was ever contemplated.

If this was what Ngatiuru did, what was their motive? In a broad sense there is no difficulty in explaining why they should want to plunder. For years the missionaries had lived among them, growing more prosperous while the tribe declined. Some £2,000 worth of property was destroyed at Whangaroa; wealth enough in European terms, but tantalizing riches to a battered tribe living on fern-root. The local chiefs had made the land available; now when they came, hoping for a meal, they were likely to be ordered off the premises for coming in the wrong way. There was no prospect of the missionaries going and no prospect of their becoming acceptable neighbours. They had not joined the tribe; they had, in effect, set up their own tribe which was steadily wearing down the authority of the Ngatiuru leadership.

Throughout the period of the mission, the three chiefs had been often on the verge of murdering the missionaries; but they had always held back. In February 1825, when the chief George was dying, the missionaries had been upset to hear that despite all the medical care they had given him, he had asked a Hokianga priest to rob the mission house as he had not had *utu* for his father having been blown up after the attack on the *Boyd*. The Hokianga man had asked if they were to be killed and he had replied no.[34] There had been no attack; but it is perhaps significant that Hika said the proposal for the Hokianga people to attack the mission station originated with Hauhau, 'the man to whom George made his will'.[35]

Since George's death, various events had occurred which may well have made the obligation to seek *utu* more urgent. One was perhaps the decomposition of George's body in the missionary coffin, although no contemporary theory to this effect has been traced. More of a possibility is the flogging of George's son. That such a theory was current for some years is shown by the following extract from Orton's journal: 'Left Mangungu for the Bay of Islands in company with Mr Hobbs. Mr H. on the way up the river related the circumstances connected with the abandonment of Whangaroa. He positively denied that it in any respect arose out of the flogging of a boy as has been currently reported; but the disagreements and wars among the natives'.[36]

This theory almost certainly originated with William Williams, who had witnessed the flogging of George's son and who repeatedly asserted that the attack was instigated by Te Puhi and his wife. Since the flogging of George himself is said to have precipitated the attack on the *Boyd*, it is very tempting to believe that the flogging of his son precipitated the other major disaster associated with the Whangaroa people.

Te Puhi's attitude towards his brother George had always been mixed. He had quarrelled with him before his death; and Te Puhi's wife was almost certainly the 'sister in law' who practised witchcraft on George, whose supporters may well have shown hostility to Te Puhi after George's death. All in all, Te Puhi may have been in such fear of his dead brother that he could have felt under particular compulsion to exact *utu* when George's son was flogged by the missionaries. In addition, there had been the rumour that George's death was due to the missionary *atua*. Finally, the missionaries had always belittled Te Puhi.

Thus, in addition to conclusive evidence that Ngatiuru participated in the attack on the mission, there are strong if not utterly conclusive indications that they engineered the attack and had powerful motives for doing so. Nor can there be any doubt that after all these years of effort, the missionaries had merely earned the enmity of the tribe they had come to convert. If this should seem an extravagant conclusion, there is one final piece of evidence—the treatment of Turner's dead child's body and Turner's own attitude to returning to New Zealand. As Turner told it, 'the ruthless barbarians' had dug up the coffin of his child, merely for the sake of the blanket in which they supposed it wrapped, and had left the remains to moulder on the surface of the earth.[37] Stack, in reporting the incident, added the rumour, which he could not confirm, that the body had been chopped to pieces.[38] If this evidence of probable desecration of the corpse is placed with the evidence of a desire for *utu* as a result of the flogging of George's son, then it is unlikely that the incident was merely an attempt to obtain another blanket.

Turner was greatly upset by the affair, and every effort was made to keep the full details from Mrs Turner. This may help explain why Turner was so reluctant to return to New Zealand and why he showed far more eagerness than Stack or Hobbs to return to Sydney. It is true that because of his young family and because he had been in charge of the mission he had been under greater strain than anyone else; but he clutched at any argument to avoid returning to New Zealand. He claimed to be useless at languages; yet in his later career showed no such disability; and his willingness to go to Tonga showed he had by no means lost his missionary enthusiasm. That his colleagues supported him in his efforts to avoid returning to New Zealand may be evidence that they knew his family was in danger. Perhaps it is significant that William Williams wrote that Te Puhi 'had a desire to strip Mr Turner and the Europeans who were with him'[39] and not simply 'a desire to strip the Europeans'.

Such speculations cannot be conclusive; but they do cast doubt on the missionaries' own explanations, which were incomplete not simply because it would have been inconvenient to tell the whole story, but also because in some areas they did not know what was happening and in other areas they could not bring themselves to admit the facts.

VII: THE SOCIAL CONTEXT OF MISSIONARY ACTIVITY

At first sight, the episode of the Whangaroa mission appears a classic confirmation of Harrison Wright's theory of the 'Maori dominance'. He saw the European impact on the Bay of Islands in the early nineteenth century taking place in three stages: initial shock, cultural assertion (the 'Maori domination'), followed by confusion and cultural breakdown. The period of dominance was marked by 'an increasing aggressiveness in the pursuit of traditional Maori goals'.[1] This self confidence, he argued, was thoroughly justified, for the Maoris could have wiped out the Europeans if they had desired. To survive in Maori society, he argued, it was necessary for anyone, whether missionary or Maori returned from foreign travel, to conform to Maori ways.

This self confidence, he concluded, was an effective barrier to alien ideas. 'As long as the Maoris were confident that what was happening to them was a matter of their own choice, as long as their culture could satisfactorily explain their experiences to them, they could scarcely be expected to change their habits of thought or ways of life.'[2] He went on to argue that acceptance of Christianity only followed in the wake of a major shift in Maori society. 'For the Maoris to turn to Christianity there had to be things happening which they could not explain in terms of their own culture and could not control by traditional means.'[3]

This theory was developed in relation to the Bay of Islands and the CMS; but it has been widely accepted as a generally descriptive term for New Zealand in this period.[4] It would appear to fit the Whangaroa episode, for apparently the missionary ideas were completely resisted and no converts were made; apparently also the Maoris were dominant, for

116

when they chose to sack the mission station there was nothing to stop them, nor was there ever any attempt to exact vengeance.

But appearances were deceptive. The next chapter will argue that despite the absence of converts, there was a significant and varied interchange of ideas in this period of apparent Maori cultural confidence. This chapter will test the theory of the Maori dominance in relation to the Whangaroa situation and, since there are no significantly distinctive features in that situation, will argue that any inadequacies to the theory in this context will indicate that the theory is not adequate in other New Zealand contexts.

The theory can be tested in three problem areas: social relationships, economic relationships, and the sanctions which controlled behaviour.

The most obvious fact about the Whangaroa tribes is that they were caught between two pressures: the social pressures of surrounding Maori tribes, and the economic pressure of the missionary presence. Both worked to corrode leadership, unity, and confidence and since both had considerable effects it is pointless to attempt to guess which was more crucial. The pressure of their neighbours was of three kinds: through trading relationships, through ceremonial occasions, such as the *Hahunga* ceremony of crying over bones of ancestors; and plundering raids. At Whangaroa these social pressures appeared to be of a negative kind, keeping the tribes in a state of uproar and making it impossible for them to benefit economically from the missionary presence. What was the point of accumulating in the missionary manner if possessions would only be plundered, or dispersed through obligatory feasting; why grow crops which would only tempt attack? Yet if such social pressures inhibited the kind of progress the missionaries thought desirable, they also had a positive role. On the one hand they ensured that leadership did not grow oppressive, since infringements of custom would provoke raiding; on the other hand they weeded out weak leadership, for if a social group could not maintain itself, it would be destroyed or dispersed among others.

In social terms therefore, the term 'dominance' hardly

seems applicable. Socially the missionaries did not dominate the Maoris for the pressures within and between tribes set limits to the influence missionaries could exert. Nor did the Maoris dominate the missionaries, even though they were subject to harrassment and were in the end plundered. It might be argued that the missionaries were under the protection of Hongi and to this extent were 'dominated'. But by now Hongi had no choice in the matter: he would not have survived if his supply of muskets had been cut off, and though missionaries no longer traded directly in muskets, their presence aided the essential European trade. Normally the missionaries could expect to be immune from plundering and to be able to set limits to their hospitality.

To some extent, it was not a unified society in which one group maintained dominance, but a plural society in which different groups went their separate ways, subject to different controls. But their ways were never completely separate; and since the separate social pressures intensified the economic difference between living standards of missionary and Maori, tension was inevitable. The missionaries were placing themselves in the classic position of the scapegoat: lacking protective force, demonstrably alien, and apparently prospering because exempt from the pressures inhibiting those around them.

In the months before the final crisis they seemed extraordinarily unaware of the danger of their position. Earlier they were much more aware, and perhaps their survival of earlier troubles had made them over-confident. In 1825, after the attack on the *Mercury*, when George was dying and there was danger of attack and talk of missionary withdrawal, the problem was the amount of time and money which had been put into the mission buildings and the amount of goods which might be lost by premature flight. At the end of the year, for example, the station had in store: 307 axes, 184 adzes, 29 spades, 300 hatchets, 410 chisels, 70 plane irons, 23 frying pans, 157 scissors, 5 billhooks, one flannel jacket, 48 iron pots, 105 hoes, 26 blankets, 12 duck trousers, and an unnumbered quantity of knives, fish-hooks, and combs.[5]

Henry Williams at this time thought the Wesleyans' predicament was an object lesson to them all not to put up such buildings in future.[6] John Hobbs also began to wonder if the mission's policy had been right. He thought that if Christ was alive and about to send missionaries to New Zealand he would not send them with the many things they now had on the mission station. 'And I think it most likely that sooner or later our lives will fall a victim to these savages in consequence of the articles of European trade which we have brought amongst them.'[7] Stack, a few days later recorded a discussion with his colleagues of whether, if they were forced to flee from the station, they should become 'native missionaries—that is live as the natives do in point of temporals'.[8]

Although this discussion appeared to arise out of their situation at that time, it is very likely that they had recently received a copy of a famous sermon delivered by the Rev. Edward Irving to the London Missionary Society on 13 May 1824, in which he urged that the modern missionary should be as Christ had urged his disciples to be: 'Therefore I say, let this type of missionary stand, that he is a man without a purse, without a scrip, without a change of raiment, without a staff, without the care of making friends or keeping friends, without the hope or desire of worldly good, without the apprehension of worldly loss, without the care of life, without the fear of death, of no rank, of no country, of no condition; a man of one thought, the gospel of Christ; a man of one purpose, the glory of God, a fool, and content to be reckoned a fool, for Christ; a madman, and content to be reckoned a madman, for Christ.'[9]

In a somewhat less exalted vein Captain Peter Dillon wrote once that it was 'highly impolitic' of bachelor missionaries in New Zealand not to choose wives 'from among the native females: as many advantages, both personal and as regards their conversion, would result from such marriages'.[10]

Against this it might be argued that involvement in the Maori kinship system might bring as many disadvantages as benefits, bringing the missionary tribal support but also tribal enemies. In any case, the suggestion ran counter to the missionary viewpoint. Hobbs's objection to the suggestion that the missionary should live among Maoris as one of them was that he would have to have a wife from England who could 'live in New Zealand in the native way and I fear there would not be many in England who could to it well as they are so astonishingly filthy'.[11] It simply did not occur to him that he might have a Maori wife.

Certainly missionary affluence and separateness created many strains, and corrupted the essentially religious message they had come to convey; cargo spoke louder than cult. Yet it can be doubted if the Maoris of this period would have taken the missionaries seriously if they had not been so manifestly well endowed with the goods of this world. Later in the century, an historian argued that their goods produced respect and added: 'The French missionaries in Canada adopted an exactly opposite system, and by becoming dependent on the aborigines, were frequently despised by them.'[12]

In economic, as in social relationships, the word dominance seems inappropriate. The Maoris certainly did not dominate the missionaries economically; the missionaries for their part were closer to a position of dominance. It fell short of dominance since the Maoris could exist without them, though in the latter period it was an existence close to starvation and in all periods missionaries were the major source of goods including weapons which had become increasingly essential to Maori existence. But perhaps the missionaries' most powerful economic pressure came not from any direct action but from their very existence as a 'reference group'—the prosperous people who altered the Maoris image of themselves. Fern root was no longer good, when missionaries dined on flour. In England at this time it was a common view that the creation of new wants would bring an aboriginal people to 'civilisation'. At Whangaroa new wants were created, but accumulation in the European manner was simply not possible in a Maori world. So, far from laying the foundations for civilization, the missionaries simply created feelings of 'relative deprivation', a revolution of rising expectations which were doomed to be frustrated.[13] There was a sense of decline, perhaps even of despair among the Maoris as the secret eluded them of the tantalizing prosperity before them. Te

Puhi at one stage said he could only learn if he lived with the missionaries: 'You are come to the island now when all the great men are dead. The present generation are but children compared with those that are gone.'[14]

The mood of the Maoris of Whangaroa by late 1826 was one of frustration. Far from taking the first confident steps to 'civilization', the chiefs veered from apathy to sudden rage, asserting themselves by acts of murder and cannibalism and then talking of abandoning their lands. Furthermore, there was a clash of generations as the young, especially those under missionary influence, scoffed at their elders, who became increasingly unsure of themselves.

In this situation, where two social groups in close proximity were experiencing increasing stress in their relations, the sanctions controlling behaviour were of crucial importance. Before European contact the Maoris had an elaborately articulated series of controls on social behaviour: marriage ties, inherited custom reinforced by religious sanctions such as the *tapu,* and a series of remedies when controls were ineffective, such as *utu* and *muru.* The missionaries were accustomed to the controls of central and local government and an established system of written law; but they were also powerfully influenced by established custom and the sanctions of religion. What happened when these two divergent traditions came into contact?

The problem is best investigated by exploring the social sanctions which came into play, to see if in fact there was simply a continuity of Maori practices. The classic definition of sanction was put forward by Radcliffe-Brown in 1934.

A sanction is a reaction on the part of a society or of a considerable number of its members to a mode of behaviour which is thereby approved (positive sanctions) or disapproved (negative sanctions). Sanctions may further be distinguished according to whether they are diffuse or organized; the former are spontaneous expressions of approval or disapproval by members of the community acting as individuals, while the latter are social actions carried out according to some traditional and recognized procedure. . . .

The sanctions existing in a community constitute motives in the individual for the regulation of his conduct in conformity with usage. . . . What is called conscience is thus in the widest sense the reflex in the individual of the sanctions of society.

Sanctions, he concluded, were 'reactions on the part of the community to events affecting its integration'.[15]

Some developments of this formulation are possible. First, a sanction does not merely operate as a reaction; the mere knowledge that it could be called into play may act as an adequate deterrent or stimulus without it ever being used. Second, although Radcliffe-Brown saw conscience as the reflex in the individual of the sanctions of society, it is possible to regard it as in itself a sanction. Finally, although Radcliffe-Brown was primarily concerned with the control of individual behaviour by the community, the theory of sanctions can fruitfully be applied to the interaction of groups within a community. (The groups are taken as within a community, for it is assumed that where social sanctions are operating, a community exists). In such an inter-group situation it is possible to think of internal and external sanctions. External sanctions are those utilized by one group in its attempt to influence the behaviour of the other group, as when missionary manipulated Maori or Maori manipulated missionary. Internal sanctions are those operating within a group to influence behaviour, whether it is inherited custom or religious belief, the pressures of conscience, or social pressures from other members of the group.

There is one other important influence on the effectiveness of sanctions in an inter-group situation; the relative prestige, or *mana*, of the groups involved. The greater the prestige of a group, the better its prospect of influencing behaviour through the use of minor, rather than serious sanctions. However, much depends on the skill with which prestige is used; at Whangaroa the potential prestige of the missionaries was used in such a way that it became humiliating; the Maoris therefore called in an extreme sanction, and the mission station was sacked.

The range of sanctions available to each group were frequently but not always duplicated on each side. They were both external and internal, although sometimes the internal sanctions could be manipulated from without. The spectrum of sanctions ranged from ultimate deterrents which exerted only vague influence, on to background pressures which set limits on behaviour, on to a series of day to day devices by which the more routine interactions were influenced.

There were two kinds of ultimate deterrent, religious and military. The missionary threat of hell fire frequently aroused uneasiness but does not appear to have affected behaviour; and missionaries, for the most part, ignored the Maori *tapu*. Fear of European military reprisal was often a more effective deterrent as the Maoris knew of the reprisals in the wake of the *Boyd* attack and had observed the soldiers and sailors on the *Dromedary* expedition at first hand. However, such reprisals were remote possibilities and, as the sacking of the mission station indicated, there were ways of spreading the responsibility of attack and thus avoiding reprisals. The missionaries for their part had no immediate counter weapon to unrestrained violence, if it was ever to be used.

Their best defence was that the cost of unrestrained violence was the ending of a relationship valuable to the Maoris; and the violence used by Maoris was usually a controlled violence, calculated to influence behaviour without provoking more dangerous reactions.[16] The missionaries to some extent used controlled violence, when involved in scuffles, or when attempting to introduce flogging as a punishment; but the Maoris used this approach more effectively, for they had devices the missionaries could not use, such as noise, or the appearance of imminent attack which never materialized, or which was kept within limits. Both sides used the reverse of violence, the threat to withdraw, or refusal to listen or communicate; and since missionaries were concerned to maintain their prestige among the Maoris and chiefs were concerned with the preservation of *mana,* this offered many ways to manipulate behaviour. Ridicule was a common weapon on both sides—a kind of non-physical violence. Although it does not appear in missionary records, more gentle forms of humour were probably frequently used by Maoris to block missionary influence.

The use of ridicule or humour was a manipulation of the

internal sanctions influencing the other. Feelings of shame powerfully controlled behaviour on both sides; but Maori *whakama* and missionary guilt were very different, though both were reinforced by the respective religious beliefs. The Maoris, living a communal existence and in the social environment they had always known, were much more susceptible to socially induced shame by means of gossip or ridicule. For the most part this worked against missionary influence, though they became susceptible to feelings of shame induced by the missionaries. The missionaries were to some extent susceptible to social pressures within their own group; there are references to 'administering reproof'. However, such pressure often produced a contrary response, as in White's reaction to Hobbs. The most powerful guilt a missionary felt, came from the workings of his own conscience. The very fact that they had left their original social environment and kin was evidence of a high resistance to continuing social pressure. But throughout their lives, through conscience, the missionaries continued to respond to pressures exerted in their childhood, and Maoris became aware that this was a way of manipulating missionary behaviour. When White was physically violent on one occasion, he recorded a Maori telling him 'that God would be angry with me for being angry with the New Zealand men and that it was a bad thing for a Missionary to be in anger. Yes! Oh *yes* it is, my God, kill the man of sin and make me meek and lowly in heart. I'm ashamed, guilty, Lord. . . .'[17]

To a limited extent, missionaries were influenced by remote pressures from their own group. There was the possibility of loss of support from England, if acceptable results were not rapidly achieved. The Maoris were more effectively limited by pressures from their own people, for example, when Hongi took the missionaries under his protection.

It has already been suggested that because of the prestige of their economic and technological success, the missionaries were in a position to operate sanctions in control of behaviour more effectively, but that they threw away this advantage by arousing resentment. Nonetheless, missionary affluence and skills inevitably acted as a powerful deterrent limiting Maori behaviour, for the Maoris feared three things: that the supply of goods and technical aid would dry up; or that it would be diverted to other tribes, or that missionaries might in some way limit the flow of goods from other Europeans. All of this altered the Maoris' image of themselves and rendered them more susceptible to influence. However, this susceptibility could turn to hostility, and aggressive behaviour could be stimulated, if missionary separateness was stressed and their affluence became demonstrably unattainable by Maoris.

This description of the complexity of sanctions operating to control behaviour may be accepted, and still it may be argued that one or other of Maori or missionary was dominant. But it is difficult to see that the concept can be usefully applied to either group. Theoretically, dominance might exist if the ultimate sanctions available to either group effectively controlled daily behaviour. But they were not effective. Religious sanctions were not effective beyond each group; although internal religious sanctions influenced behaviour within each group. Ultimate military sanctions were usually thought remote and evadable, and in any case they were likely to mean the end of a relationship thought desirable on both sides. A deterrent is useless if it leaves nobody to deter. It was noteworthy that although in the end the Maoris used extreme measures against mission property, they only used controlled violence against the missionaries themselves: they were frightened away but not harmed. It would be interesting to know which sanction most protected them. The normal and most effective sanctions were the minor sanctions controlling day to day situations and these were directed, not at dominance which produces all manner of counter pressures, but at acceptable behaviour in a continuing relationship.

This range of sanctions was far greater than in the pre-European situation; and some of the pre-European sanctions did not operate in this new relationship. In many respects the missionaries, and other Europeans, are best thought of as an additional tribal grouping, but they made significant alterations to the methods of inter-tribal adjustment. Probably the two most important groups of sanctions in pre-European society were those associated with marriage and religion.[18]

Missionaries, unlike many other Europeans, did not marry Maoris, and so denied themselves the kin-group protection that went with marriage; and they attempted to deny themselves the protection of Maori religious sanctions, while unsuccessfully attempting to introduce new religious sanctions. (There appears to have been a certain religious awe associated with the missionaries but it appears to have been more Maori than Christian.) But if the missionaries threw away many possible protective sanctions, as Europeans they carried with them powerful new sanctions: the background threat of military or naval reprisal and all the sanctions associated with a more powerful economy and technology which was becoming essential for survival in inter-tribal conflicts. It was no longer an exclusively 'Maori world'.

Since, therefore, the situation at Whangaroa was one where multiple sanctions existed to control the behaviour of all groups involved, the concept of 'dominance', whether it be Maori or European, is inappropriate. The term 'dominance' in this context appears to come from the writings of Ralph Linton.[19] It is worth remembering, therefore, that it did not originate in a study of a Polynesian situation, for it is tempting to believe that there are qualities in Polynesian social traditions which prevent social encounters being fought out in terms of dominance and submission, the interaction of polar opposites, one of which must prevail. Linton's analysis proceeds by the interaction of such opposites: dominance-submission, equality-inequality, superiority-inferiority; and this was to carry over into Wright's book about New Zealand.

There are strong pressures on any writers dealing with contact situations to think in terms of opposites, for contact is usually seen as the interaction of two separate entities. This tendency is reinforced in two ways. First, in any attempt to resolve a confused situation it is a very natural tendency to try and reduce the choice to two possibilities; by definition the term 'alternative' is restricted to a choice of two. Second, in the background of writing about contact situations is an older tradition, the rhetoric of missionary propaganda, which is full of polar opposites, whether describing a religious or a social condition. Thus, missionary writing moves between the two religious extremes of Christian-heathen, converted-pagan, saved-damned, pious-depraved, godly-ungodly; between the racial extremes of white and black; between the social extremes of civilized-savage, advanced-primitive. Our own age changes the terminology in the hope of avoiding ethnocentricity; we talk of complex-simple, large-scale small-scale, Europeanized-traditional, modernized-underdeveloped. But we merely alter the language without altering the underlying modes of thought.

If we assume two entities, Maori and European, completely separate, then it is natural to assume that one or other must be 'dominant', or if we select less stark language, 'in a stronger position'. But if we examine the encounters that take place after the initial encounter, it is extremely rare to find one side exclusively European and the other exclusively Maori. There were Europeans who became Pakeha-Maoris; Maoris who became *Mihanere* Maoris; there were relationships arising from commerce, co-habitation, or religion; and Maoris were ever ready to use Europeans in inter-tribal conflicts or Europeans to seek Maori support. As this chapter has demonstrated, once Europeans were present, there was no longer an exclusively Maori culture; equally, it was impossible for Europeans to transmit their culture in its entirety. They shed much in migrating; much, as individuals, they had never known; and in settling they absorbed much from their new physical as well as social environment. As has frequently been pointed out, people not cultures come into contact; and if the word culture is unsatisfactory in this context so also it is clear that significant social contacts involved more than two groups and that the range of responses to contacts covered a wider spectrum than simply a choice between dominance and submission. A further example of such a spectrum of reactions will be given in the next chapter.

VIII: THE EXCHANGE OF IDEAS

Interaction takes place whenever there is contact and it can be expected that ideas will be exchanged in a manner resembling every other exchange. At Whangaroa, where multiple sanctions maintained an uneasy social equilibrium, there was a considerable two-way flow of ideas, which were accepted or rejected in a variety of ways. This does not mean, as Wright appears to argue, that social conditions determined the reception of ideas; that while 'dominant', Maoris rejected missionary teaching and when 'demoralized' accepted it. If it is desired to follow such social determinism, the Whangaroa evidence would seem to suggest a contrary conclusion. In the early period of the mission, in Wright's terminology, the Maoris could be termed confident; there was little internal conflict or external pressure and this was the period when they listened most when missionaries preached, began observing the *tapu* of the sabbath, erecting church buildings. Then pressures built up; leadership was challenged from within, pressures mounted from without; the contrast with missionary affluence became more and more evident and intolerable. By then the missionaries were more experienced and at least a little more coherent in their use of the Maori language; but they were rejected. It could be argued, quite convincingly, that when socially disorganized, the Maoris were too demoralized to experiment with new religious ideas.

It is too easy to argue that social conditions determine ideas, for every society has elements of stability and of disintegration, any of which can be taken as relating to ideology. The observer can select his evidence to fit his case; and if it is difficult to establish objective truth of social conditions, so also it is difficult to establish that large numbers of people have genuinely changed or retained an ideology. Furthermore, this chapter will demonstrate that when ideas are exchanged, social conditions are not the only determining influences.[1]

Both missionaries and Maoris at Whangaroa were at some disadvantage in the exchange of ideas. The Maoris' disadvantage was that although they had their own religious beliefs, the debate seems to have followed the themes that were significant to the missionary religion. Possibly our view would be different if we had Maori records to supplement those of the missionaries; but on the evidence we have, the debate seems to have centred around the nature of God or the gods, the creation, fall, and redemption of man; the resurrection, the judgement, and the future world; and although for many of these topics there was an alternative Maori explanation, their grouping was in terms of missionary understanding.

On the other hand, the missionaries were at a considerable disadvantage in having to express themselves in Maori, using words with different connotations. For example, they took over the word *atua* to describe their own God. Sometimes they distinguished their own God as the '*atua nui*', or great God. This might not have mattered if *atua* was an equivalent word. But the missionaries found the Maori concept extremely confusing.

First of all, they concluded the 'the New Zealanders have no Idea whatever of our spiritual and supreme God'.[2] But the word *atua* was used in many ways. It might refer to figures of mythology, like Maui, the first man, who hooked up the fish of New Zealand; or 'Ena' (Hine or Hina), whom White described as 'a Female' by whom evil was introduced into the world.[3] Or, according to missionary accounts, it might refer to any animal, thing, or person inspiring dread or awe. Thus the word was applied to chiefs, or even to missionaries. 'Alas poor deluded Creatures, they think any person raised above the common people is deified', wrote Turner.[4] Or it might refer to someone who had eaten human flesh, or to a dead body.[5] Most frequently the word applied to a departed spirit[6] which might enter a fish, a reptile, or a bird.[7] At sea, such a spirit might be a *taniwha* which could enter a shark or a porpoise,[8] which might come to the water's edge and enter the *ngarara* or lizard and kill people.[9] Stack was told such a spirit might descend from the sky to a lizard.[10] There were similar beliefs about stars. When anyone died, it was believed that the left eye became a star, the bright stars the eyes of great men, the dim ones of slaves.[11] When a comet passed over, there were various explanations, including the view that the missionary's Jehovah had come over from Europe.[12]

Atua were believed to be largely responsible for disease. The exact details are not clear from missionary accounts. On one occasion they were told that a stone from the other world had been placed in the bowels of the sick chief George.[13] When a missionary 'blister' was placed on a sick man's chest and later burst, the water that ran down was taken to be the *atua*. More often they were told that the *atua* itself was eating the insides of the sick person.[14] But although sickness could be caused by the malevolence of the *atua*—as also by the malevolence of someone practising witchcraft—it was not necessarily so. White quoted the case of a sick chief who attributed his illness to a spirit of a dead young man who loved him and wished the chief to join him in the other world where there were plenty of good things to enjoy.[15]

The missionaries were soon incorporated into this pattern of belief. The new diseases which came with the European were attributed to the missionaries' *atua;* whenever missionaries fell sick they were thought afflicted with an *atua.*[16] The missionaries attempted to counter these beliefs with their own theological belief that death and disease entered the world as a result of the fall of man.[17]

There is no evidence that this provoked any response; but the Maoris were prepared to incorporate aspects of the European world into their own framework of ideas. Thus, when chief George lay dying, his brother made a great noise and fired off several muskets to frighten the evil spirits away.[18] George himself asked the missionaries to look into their books for some medicine to do him good and later asked them 'to pray to Jesus Christ to take the God out of his belly'.[19]

There are occasional references to the word *wairua*, which at various times the missionaries interpreted as meaning 'spirit'.[20] In their understanding of the word, *wairua* seems to have been generally interchangeable with *atua*. Frequently the missionaries simply reported Maori beliefs about 'spirits', with no indication of what Maori word was used, or of what concept was involved.

They reported many beliefs about spirits: for example, it might be said of a sick person that his or her spirit had fled, or that they had a new spirit.[21] A spirit might also be called back from the invisible world by the efforts of a Maori priest.[22] Departed spirits also returned without being summoned, and for this reason food such as a pigeon might be hung on a bush for a spirit to feed on.[23] Similarly, departed spirits might return in the night and by whistling convey news from the other world.[24] It was on such evidence that some Maoris claimed that Christian Rangi, the first man officially baptized by the CMS had gone, not to the Christian heaven, but to the Maori other world, the *Reinga*.[25] Such beliefs were not too far removed from missionary belief in ministering angels.

When a chief died, a slave might be killed, or a wife might commit suicide that their spirit might accompany his to the other world; and his muskets might be placed with his his body that their spirits might accompany him.[26] To prove to the missionaries that every person had a spirit, the evidence of a reflection in a looking glass was used. To prove that objects had spirits, at least two arguments were used. First there was the noise given off by two objects banged together;[27] then there was the evidence of the shadow. The missionaries ridiculed this: 'we referred them to a pole standing by us and asked them if it had not a shadow. They said it had. We then asked them whether it could see, whether it could speak feel taste and talk, to which they replied it could not. We then asked them whether if they took a corpse and set it in an erect posture it would not have a shadow too and that it could neither hear speak smile taste nor see, and this was in consequence of the spirits having taken its departure. They looked earnestly and felt the weight of the argument and repeated some of the observations over again among themselves and fully gave up the point. Having sung and prayed with them we returned home to dinner'.[28]

The missionaries also tried to ridicule the evidence of dreams; for where missionaries appealed to the authority of the Bible, the Maoris appealed to their dreams, believing, for example, that while asleep a man's spirit might wander to the spirit world, the details of which were thus thoroughly familiar to them. The reason why missionaries did not know about the Maori spirit world was because they did not have dreams. 'They had much to say in favour of their dreams, and said the reason why we speak of *Hell Fire* is because we do not go to the Reinga; as they do in their sleep. This we soon convinced them was a falsehood, and related one of our dreams which silenced their objection. They made many laughable mistakes.'[29]

Dreams were also important in foretelling the future. Stack described many 'prognostications'. If a rat came out of the bush and near the fire, it foretold that someone would soon die and be laid on the spot; if the instep of the foot itched, someone was talking of you at a distance; if the tips of the fingers itched, it foretold you would soon eat fish and be pricked by the bone in the fingers. If a man dreamt he entered a house and found all the doors closed when he wanted to leave, it foretold his death by violence; if he dreamt he had snared a rat, or if he dreamt he had gone fishing and filled his net, he would be murdered. If before a battle he dreamt he gathered a large number of birds and they were not inclined to peck at him, he would take many slaves; if they did, he would be destroyed by the enemy.[30]

Since dreams had such significance, it was probably a mistake for the missionaries to belittle them, for it was in dreams that the first hints came that missionary ideas were taking root. The chief Kearoa, for example, told them of a dream where he saw Jesus Christ hanging on the Cross, while he stood at the foot of it. 'He looked down upon *me*. There was a strange white man who took me by the hand and wanted to guide me up, but I was afraid. . . .'[31] Another reported a conversation with a sleeping man before any white people came to New Zealand: 'He said he saw an immense fire as large as from the North Cape to the River Thames and that this great fire was close to the Heavens and had immensely large Doors or Gates that it was filled with persons some New Zealanders and some Englishmen who were all Butting their Heads into the Flames while they walked on their hands and knees. He said also that he had a *companion* who saw much but was lost in the scene not being able to fly. Now said he I am a Ma-a-ra-re that is "a flying thing". Now by this circumstance I know that what you white People say about Hell is true.'[32] Turner also wrote of a young man who, after instruction, told of seeing the flames of hell in a dream.[33]

Against this background of unbelief, and given the missionaries' inadequate command of language, there were many possibilities of subtly misunderstanding the nature of the new God to whom the missionaries gave the familiar name of *atua*. Hobbs, for example, was asked if this *atua* 'was like the Atua Maodi that is like the departed spirits of native men'.[34] On another occasion, Hobbs stressed that his God, whose name was Jehovah, 'had never had a corporeal Body and consequently was different in nature from the spirits of mankind after death whom they call Gods or Atua and that this Atua whose name is Jehovah made all things and would after death call us to an account for our actions while in the world, that he was angry with us for our evil and would forgive our sins if we could believe that His son Jesus Christ died in our stead or as our substitutes to satisfy his wrath with a few other plain things of good tendency'.[35] He also told them departed spirits were not gods; there was but one God and 'the King of England the Governor of Port Jackson and all the great men in the world were but servants of *Jehovah* neither were New Zealanders anything else'.[36]

One of the commonest questions about this new God was where was he? If one prayed to him, could he hear at a distance?[37] Was he yonder at the missionaries' house?[38] The missionaries gave conflicting answers to this unaccustomed question. On one occasion White replied that God was everywhere and knew everything. His listeners objected that if God was everywhere, why did they not see him? Let them see and they would believe. 'I directed their attention to the wind and asked if they could see it. This argument at once silenced them, but still they endeavoured to turn all that we said into

Obscenity and ridicule. I told them that we had come to tell them about Jesus Christ who died to save them and if they would not attend to our instructions but continue in their ignorance and die in that state that they would go to a great fire and burn for ever, etc. Some of their countenances changed and they desisted from their vile conversation. This being the first time that we had visited this Tribe.'[39]

There were different missionary answers to the question of where exactly this *atua* was. Stack, for example, said 'His presence was confined to *no* place but that he was even in their hearts'.[40] The statement that Jehovah was everywhere, provoked the query, why didn't he sink if he was on the sea?[41] Hobbs stated confidently that Jehovah lived beyond the stars 'and made them together with the Sun and Moon. We also told them that he made the fish of the sea and gave them to Man for food together with an abundance of fine fruits. And here came to the fall but could not interest them with the Recovery'.[42] Heckled by some of Hongi's followers to say where Jesus Christ was, Hobbs, after a moment of confusion, replied that he was everywhere, covering the earth and filling the heavens and listening to what they said. 'By this time a solemn respect seemed to manifest itself in most of their countenances.'[43]

Since Maoris so frequently saw *atua* themselves, it seems that they found it difficult to credit an *atua* which the missionaries could not also claim to have seen themselves.[44] Despite all missionary efforts, the Maoris still tended to conceive of the missionary God as a familiar *atua*. An old woman, for example, told Hobbs she had seen the spirit of Jehovah and it resembled a shadow. Hobbs told her she was a great liar and it was the devil at work in her heart. She altered her tone, not wishing to give offence, he wrote.[45]

But what was the nature of this *atua*? Like the missionaries themselves he must have seemed alternatively loving and angry.[46] How was it, if this new *atua* was both loving and all powerful, the same or worse calamities seemed to be befalling them since the missionaries came: crops spoilt by rain or drought or the attacks of their enemies, more people dying of disease; and all this although they had learnt to keep the *tapu* of the Sabbath? Either the new *atua* was causing this trouble or he was failing to prevent other *atua*.[47]

The devil aroused considerable interest. Who made him? Did he live in the same place as Jehovah?[48] Why had Jehovah not prevented Satan from overcoming Adam and Eve?[49] Was the devil also omnipresent?[50] Such questions led on to doctrines concerning the Creation and Fall of Man. In order to gain acceptance for their own views, the missionaries had to refute the story of Maui 'their first man', who had fished up the fish of New Zealand from the sea. White described such a discussion. 'The account of the creation very much interested the Chief and People. Tepere called Adam *Dust* and Eve *Bone,* in the midst of our discussion, he interrupted us by saying that everything came from Maue etc I asked him if the land etc was really hooked up by Maue, to which he answered yes, then there was no *Timber* before he hooked it up? No. Where then did he stand etc? In a Canoe, where did he get the canoe?' At this there was a roar of laughter and they acknowledged ignorance, according to White.[51]

There is no missionary evidence of reciprocal mockery of the story of the creation of Adam and Eve, or of the fall of man. Instead, there were fairly factual questions. Would the world be as it is if only Eve had sinned?[52] Would perhaps only women have gone to hell?[53] 'Was there any night in Paradise? Did our first parents wear clothes at night? If our first parents had not eaten the forbidden fruit what likeness would men have? Would there be no old age? . . .'[54] If Adam had not sinned, would the New Zealanders have known of Jehovah?[55] The story of the Creation does not appear to have aroused any particular resistance, although one man argued 'that man had been from all eternity and that a succession would continue to all eternity'.[56] But not only was the rival creation myth of Maui apparently readily abandoned, there were several instances of local Maoris repeating the missionaries' account to visiting Maoris.[57] Questions about the creation led on to the question did matter exist before the creation, or was all vacuity?[58]

The fall of man and his redemption by Christ's sacrifice on the cross, does, however, appear to have presented more difficulties. As seen, a frequent question on the fall of man was why did God not prevent Satan from tempting man?[59] The doctrine of the atonement presented particular difficulties. As Hobbs put it, his knowledge of the language would not enable him to explain Christ's atonement in any satisfactory way, 'especially as the New Zealanders have no idea of their accountability to Jehovah nor wish to believe the testimony given concerning their fallen state'.[60]

As far as the missionaries themselves were concerned, the doctrine that Christ had died for all men was of particular significance; this, as much as anything, accounted for their missionary vocation. White, for example, described their errand to New Zealand as 'to be able to tell the wretched creatures by whom we are surrounded that *Christ* died for them and to invite them to partake of the Blessings of his saving grace'.[61] Nathaniel Turner spoke of 'the Doctrine of General Redemption' as one on which 'my soul ever delights to dwell'.[62] Their hearers did not always share his concern for all humanity. When White said he wished all New Zealanders might hear his teaching, one man responded jestingly: 'Oh . . . let them go to Hell they are a bad tribe.'[63] Many of these concepts were alien to their hearers: the idea that man was accountable to his God for his sins and the notion of vicarious sacrifice—even the notion of sacrifice itself—was apparently not significantly developed among Maoris.

The missionaries tried to explain their doctrines in Maori terms, and subtly altered them in the process. The plucking of forbidden fruit by Adam became a breach of *tapu,* for which the Christian *atua* would have exacted *utu* but for the sacrifice of Christ.[64] The missionaries themselves were mystified by the concept of *utu,* whereby someone quite innocent of an infraction might suffer the penalty.[65] In due course, it became a convenient way of explaining the atonement. But that missionary ideas were being absorbed into a very different framework was shown when a boy asked why nails were not sacred since they fastened the body of Christ to the cross?[66] Here, as in the keeping of the *tapu* of the Sabbath, the Maoris were prepared to follow the letter of any possible commandments much more literally than the missionaries themselves.

The other main group of ideas concerned life after death. At the northern tip of New Zealand was the area now known as Cape Reinga, and from here the spirits of the dead left for the other world, which was known to the people of Whanga-roa as either the *Reinga* or the *Po*.[67] The Maoris knew about this in great detail for various reasons. They went there and returned in their dreams; departed spirits returned and talked to them in the night; and those who lived near the north of New Zealand could often see the departing spirits, and from this tell whether there had been a great battle among the Bay of Islanders or the manner of the spirit's death. If his head had been split with a tomahawk, one would stick to the spirit's head; if stabbed, a knife would be in its side, or if roasted, hot stones and sticks would be attached to him till he arrived in the other world 'where his friends would relieve him of such burdens and inconveniences'. Using the weapon of ridicule, the missionaries asked, what if his head was cut off? and were assured he would still have a head.[68]

The Maori *Reinga* differed from the missionaries' other world in several ways. For one thing it was down below, whereas the missionary Heaven was up above. 'Speaking to old Kuki on where his spirrit would go if he died he said down to the (reinga) or invisible world. I smiled. Well (said he) which way do you say the spirrit goes? I told him the spirrit of a good man went up to Heaven. What (said he) at noon day can you see the spirrit ascending there?'[69] Hobbs was told that when the sun went down or the moon disappeared, it went to enlighten the world of spirits, and that when the tide ebbed, it flowed to them.[70]

The Maori spirit world also differed from that of the mis-sionaries in that there was no division, with the wicked sent to eternal torment and the good to everlasting bliss, for, wrote Turner, 'they think they are all good, and that when they die they shall go to a fine country and have plenty of sweet potatoes, etc, etc'.[71] As one old chief put it, he 'would not go to Heaven, nor would he go to Hell to have nothing but fire to eat, but would go to the *Raing* or *Po,* to eat *kumaras* sweet potatoes with his friends who had gone before'.[72] With his highly developed sense of kinship the Maori could not accept, as the missionaries apparently could, that one's friends or relatives might have been assigned to eternal woe. Old chief Te Puhi, when asked who would save his soul after death, replied that he had plenty of relations in the invisible world and that he had been told by those who had been there that a house was prepared for him. 'Of all the natives in the valley, there is hardly one seems to have a more besotted soul than Tepui', wrote Stack.[73]

Once again the missionaries tried the weapon of ridicule. If the other world was such a pleasant place, why did they strive to stay alive, even sending for missionary medicine? Why did they not hang themselves? 'This irony was too strong for them, they were confused and held their peace.'[74]

One final contrast was the difference between the missionary and the Maori concept of eternal bliss. 'Of pure spiritual pleasures', wrote Turner, 'they have no conception, their Heaven is all in carnal delights'.[75] In both groups, notions of the spirit world reflected the values and attitudes of this world.

The Maori spirit world also kept pace with changes in this world. Since muskets were desirable, they were available in the other world.[76] Europeans were also incorporated: as in the news that the dead chief George had been carried by a boat's crew of H.M.S. *Dromedary* on board ship and given a miraculous cure;[77] and that he had three European wives.[78] When Turner challenged them on their belief that there would be plenty of European goods, ships, muskets, etc, in the other world, they replied, 'that their future residence was near the white People's and that they had these things from them'.[79] Economic dependence on the European was apparently so much taken for granted in this world that it was transferred to the spirit world. But since the spirit world was in both cases an imaginative extension of this world, the Maoris found as much to ridicule in the missionaries' notions of the Resurrection, Heaven, and Hell, as the missionaries found in the Maori spirit world.

As has been seen when missionaries were invited to a Maori *tangi* or the subsequent *hahunga* ceremony, they would usually try to preach their doctrines of the Resurrection, namely 'that the Book of Jehovah would destroy this earth and that when it should come to an end these Bones which they saw should again be fitted together and clothed with flesh, skin, etc . . .' some destined for Heaven, some for Hell.[80] Not surprisingly they received little response on these occasions for the close relatives were overcome with grief and the others given over to merriment; and the general noise was hardly conducive to close theological argumentation. As Hobbs put it: 'I endeavoured to preach to them the Resurrection but they received it as one who had been in a dream.'[81] Nonetheless there were questions about the doctrine of physical resurrection. A frequent question was, what became of the victims of cannibalism? Was it reasonable to expect that 'a body which had been eaten first next become excrement, and lastly become the food of maggots', would be gathered again and raised to life?[82]

This emphasis on physical resurrection, and the further missionary statement that whoever was saved would have eternal life, was at first misinterpreted as a statement that believers, or even all white men, would not suffer physical death. When it was apparent that white people did in fact die, as did Turner's child, there were questions and missionaries had to clarify what they meant.[83]

The doctrine of the Final Judgement helped create the image of Jehovah as a God of anger, and this also must have been the mental image of Christ. When the missionaries felt angry with the Maoris, it was all too easy to assure their hearers that Christ was angry with them. A man who had killed and was about to eat a slave, was assured that the *atua nui* was angry with him, that both he and the body about to be consumed would rise again from the dust, to stand before the judgement seat of Christ.[84] Those who worked on the Sabbath, the *ra tapu,* were assured that God or Christ was angry with them, and could see them even if the missionaries could not;[85] and the missionaries did nothing to discourage the idea that damage to crops was the consequence of Christ's vengeance for the breach of *tapu.*[86] Since the Maoris had not been in the habit of calculating the days of the week in the European manner this presented difficulties.

But the *tapu* of the Sabbath was usually one of the earliest missionary ideas to be absorbed; and the Maoris were very upset to find that even when they kept this *tapu,* the angry Jehovah, or Christ, still caused newly planted potatoes to die in the ground.[87]

The main point of difference over the doctrine of the Judgement, was that the missionaries thought in terms of individual salvation and this idea had little attraction for the Maoris. God, said Hobbs, would single each out and reward him individually for his works and on this occasion claimed attentive hearers.[88] But when asked who would take care of their souls after death, Maoris usually replied, their relatives; or that they would escape in the crowd.[89] Yet another reply to the question, 'Where will you go when Jehovah comes and the world is all on fire?' was 'I'll run away'.[90]

This same note of shrewd practicality was evident in the questions asked—such specific questions that missionaries, we may guess, were probably led into much more detailed descriptions than they intended. Stack, for example, held forth on the destruction of the world by fire and was asked where the ships would sail? 'To which I replied that houses as well as ships would all be destroyed. How is it said he that the fire which will destroy the ships and houses will not the men also. This I was enabled to answer in a measure to his satisfaction. "Will not the flames of the burning world reach up to the righteous and burn them" said he.'[91] When Puru, or 'Jackey', of Toropapa tried to pass on the missionary teachings to other Maoris they were sceptical of the idea of the destruction of the world by fire, challenging him to take a firebrand and set the sea alight.[92] Missionary teaching about heaven did not seem to evoke many questions, although Hobbs was asked with genuine interest whether there were plenty of pigs in heaven?[93] A fairly common comment was that it was a place for white men but not for Maoris.[94] They were also asked if the people of the sky would not fight with them if they went up there?[95]

Hell, on the other hand, which shared with the *Reinga* the characteristic of being down below, was a different matter and the missionaries were soon giving it a local context by com-

paring it to New Zealand thermal areas.[96] It was given a
Maori name, *kapura nui* (large fire), and missionary emphasis
on hell fire led to the reaction 'that Jesus Christ is a red god
like fire'.[97]

But in the discussion of hell, the difference between the two
kinds of mind was illustrated. The missionary, who acquired
his notion of hell from a book, rather than the world of sense
experience, tried to evoke a mood of horror by abstract meta-
phor, dealing with symbols that were so much a part of his
culture that he no longer visualized the actual reality. For the
missionary, darkness evoked fear and flames evoked fear;
hence if hell was a place of fear it was both dark and fiery.
The Maori, partly because his world of experience was
more concrete, and partly because he was encountering these
ideas for the first time, would ask such questions as, how
could hell be dark if there were flames?[98]

One young woman could only comprehend the idea in
terms of prosaic fact, asking 'Will the skin peel off in Hell.
She said if the skin did not peel off, never mind being red
hot. Alas! Alas! "Who can dwell with fiends in everlasting
burnings" ', wrote Stack.[99] The same note of practicality was
found in the response to the statement that the bulk of mankind went to the flames: 'Then if the greater number go to
Hell we will be the greatest in number and will go and take
away the kingdom from Jehovah.'[100]

The missionary other world could not be made to correspond with the Maori world of everyday experience. It
ignored the obligations of kinship, it held no delights for a
warrior people, and it could not be described in terms of
practical experience as the Maori knew it. Only with the
mental transformations that came with literacy would such
concepts begin to appear intelligible.

These examples of the ways in which ideas were exchanged,
suggest various conclusions. The main reaction on both sides
was to reject the views of the other. Yet, as could be expected
from other studies,[101] rejection is never complete. There was
in fact a wide range of reactions, the analysis of which gives
a greater accuracy than the simple contrast of the polar
opposites, 'heathen' and 'converted'.

Rejection certainly was the major response, and among Maoris this was mainly because of the strangeness of missionary ideas and the difficulty of reconciling these with significant aspects of Maori existence. The missionaries themselves must have appeared strange in many ways: they had sharp noses, they did not eat fern root, they wore different clothes, they lacked strength, their women were tender. Above all they lacked fluency in the Maori language. Missionaries were not warriors but they must still have appeared harsh. When Turner lectured the chief Te Puhi on the need to beat children who misbehaved, the old chief 'appeared quite disgusted and said we were an *iwi kino,* a bad tribe'.[102] When the wife of the dead chief George made several attempts to kill herself, Te Puhi was told white women would not do this and replied, 'You white people have no love'.[103] There were many comments that the missionaries were mean in their trading and unfriendly in their restrictions on Maori access to the mission station.[104]

But this attempt to maintain, in effect, the purity and integrity of mission premises, was only one manifestation of a contrast in attitudes which occurred again and again. The Maoris lived in close proximity to nature; the missionaries, by their clothing and housing, by husbanding their resources, planned their lives so that the forces of nature were controlled or kept at bay. The Maoris practised polygamy, lived in wider informal social groups, allowing their children to develop freely in the community as a whole. Missionaries believed in one husband, one wife, or in unmarried chastity; they were prepared to forsake their kin to live at the other end of the world, but they believed that children should be closely controlled by the two parents, preserved from the corruption of wider society. One way was the way of acceptance, whether of nature or of society; the other was the way of continual choice, preserving the pure, rejecting the impure. The Maoris lived in a society in which their concepts of the sacred entered into every social relationship;[105] the missionaries came from a secularizing society in which their religion could only be preserved in the small exclusive family.

There is no evidence that the missionaries ever glimpsed

that the inter-relationship of religion and social structure complicated their problem, or paused to consider whether Christianity could break loose from its association with the small family. The small family unit of the missionaries produced pressures unknown in the wider social units of the Maori: constant and consistent parental concern for the child's emotional, intellectual, and moral development; a constant manipulation of behaviour by emphasizing restraint of natural passion and by fostering a sense of guilt and striving. Missionary views on the discipline and nurture of children were closely enmeshed with their family structure; so also were their views on what constituted sexual morality. The economic attitudes they sought to convey: the concepts of regulated hours of work for the purpose of accumulating and preserving possessions, all assumed the absence of extended kinship obligations and of concepts such as *mana, utu,* and *muru,* all of which ran counter to extensive material accumulation in the European manner. It is difficult to avoid the conclusion that of all the issues in debate in the Maori-missionary encounter, the nature of the family unit was the most crucial, for most other issues were influenced by it.

The contrast was stark; and where missionaries were so clearly different, it was a natural conclusion that their religion went with a whole pattern of alien behaviour and was not for Maoris. While the rejection was often outright— 'obscenity and ridicule'—sometimes it was rejected politely— 'I shall think about it before I reject it'[106]—or with the statement that perhaps a future generation would understand.

Occasionally, the missionaries encountered a natural sceptic, as with the man who 'did not attempt to defend the common notions but asked who in the world could tell what becomes of the spirit of man after death'.[107] Others, while unable to accept the missionary teaching, nonetheless, under pressure of missionary ridicule, became ashamed of their own beliefs. Sometimes the missionary teaching, while still not accepted, aroused fear. This was particularly so when the missionary God was seen as a vengeful *atua.* An old woman complained of being speared by Jesus Christ.[108] Various people thought they saw the white people's atua—'this thing we see sometimes black and sometimes white dressed in European clothing'.[109] The name given this god, who was said to have caused various deaths, including that of the chief George, was *'turore'*, a word which Stack said derived from 'Tu to stop and rore the brain', and which he thought came into use as a result of a 'Brain fever' which carried off many people after the cutting off of the *Boyd*.[110]

These were all variations of a reaction which was basically one of rejection. But at the same time, there were two other reactions. Firstly, there was 'compartmentalization', best seen in the approach to disease, where there was Maori illness for which the *tohunga* was appropriate and the new Pakeha diseases, for which the missionary was appropriate; or in the behaviour of the children who were fairly European on the mission station but completely Maori when they went home.

Secondly, there was 'fusion' or 'syncretism', which came in various ways. Reports of dreams indicated the infiltration of missionary ideas about hell and about Jesus Christ. The technology associated with the missionaries' culture—firearms, metal tools, European clothes, methods of agriculture, literacy, and missionary medicine—all were accepted where they could be used in a Maori context, without any necessary acceptance of missionary religious teaching. Sometimes this willingness to accept took the form of imitation, in which the element of fashion probably entered. Turner reported a man saying 'if he had such clothes as we had he should understand as we do. . . .'[111] Although this incident suggested missionary prestige, there were probably aspects of missionary life and conduct that enjoyed a temporary vogue simply for their own sake.

A variation of 'fusion' was to learn without understanding the European connotations. Prayers would be learnt as *karakia* and were much more popular than sermonizing. 'The *discoursing* on spiritual things appears to these poor creatures of little weight in competition with a form of words addressed to him who desires the *Heart* as well as the lips', wrote Stack.[112] One of the boys in the mission household told Stack that they imitated the missionaries but that was all.[113] In all these examples of fusion the ideas were absorbed into a Maori mental framework, the clearest instance being the keeping of the *tapu* of the Sabbath.

As far as the missionaries themselves were concerned, they also rejected Maori ways and ideas and yet, without realizing it, they were influenced. They learnt to tone down unwelcome aspects of their teaching: for example, in hell fire sermonizing, Stack wrote of trying to avoid stirring up 'an improper feeling in the native mind'.[114] It was extremely rare for missionaries to concede that in any respect Maori ways were better than European; but there was one such passage in Hobbs's journal, written after a visit from Thomas Kendall, the lapsed CMS missionary. He contrasted the two methods of child rearing. In England, where the mother's reason was 'fatally perverted by the tide of custom', she kept the infant over-clad and breathing 'the unwholesome stench of a close room', so that the baby cried and raved for breath to save its life; cramming it with food and physic which often terminated its existence in convulsions. In New Zealand, the infant, fed as God intended, breathed the pure air, free of clothes or bandages. There was much else in this vein, contrasting the food and drink of the two countries, and contrasting the Maori, who enjoyed all the pleasure of animal life which a vigorous mind could enjoy, with the poor Englishman 'who if not under the cheering influence of his favourite poison like an oyster without eyes or ears incapable of enjoying life', was often driven to end his miserable existence.[115] Hobbs ended by praising the industry of his countrymen, in contrast to what he considered Maori idleness; nonetheless it was a rare and glowing tribute to a way of life he had come to change. It is possible that the missionaries were more often favourably impressed by Maori life than the written record would indicate.

A more subtle influence lay in the process of translation. A limited command of the Maori language meant that they taught only what they had learnt to express; and they tended to learn from other Europeans or from Kendall's grammar. Preaching among the Maori tended to be restricted to Sundays and other occasions of contact were fairly restricted. There was also the difficulty of expressing their ideas through

the use of Maori words (such as *atua, karakia, tapu,* etc.)
with different connotations in the original language; or of
using Maori concepts to explain somewhat different theological ideas: for example, *utu* in explaining the atonement, or
local examples to dramatize concepts such as hell.

They were also influenced by the process of question and
answer. As they were asked unexpected questions, so they
expounded a different message. They were faced with a people
who did not take for granted teachings they had themselves
accepted as part of their cultural heritage; who wanted
abstract ideas spelt out in concrete detail; who appealed to
the evidence of the senses rather than a literary tradition:
could you see, taste, feel, hear? If this influenced the emphasis
of missionary teaching, so also contempt and ridicule led to
an emphasis on a God of anger, although this was perhaps
more a consolidation of an existing tendency in the missionary
approach. To some extent the missionaries seem to have learnt
that this emphasis was unwise. Their own accounts confirm
that although hell-fire threats could impress, they could also,
as travellers such as Augustus Earle noted later, arouse
ridicule.

Another missionary reaction to rejection was to rely less
on the intrinsic merits of their teachings and more on the
prestige of European skills and technology. Medicine became
a latter-day gift of miracles to open the way for the gospel;
and emphasis was placed on the tangible benefits of peace
and prosperity, which it was claimed, would follow in the
wake of baptism. At this point it could be asked whether they
were missionaries of religion or of English culture. But the
final reaction to rejection, was to place more and more
emphasis on pioneering and less on preaching, developing
their farms and gardens and premises and abandoning the
schools and preaching which were winning no response.

Thus, both among Maoris and missionaries, although rejection was the major response, it was accompanied on each
side by fusion and by compartmentalization; and rejection in
itself often prompted adjustments in the position of the other
party. In the warfare of ideas, as in actual fighting, com-
batants learn from each other and in their conflict become

more, not less, similar. There were no 'conversions', but this does not mean there was no exchange of ideas.

The exchange of ideas took place in a social context and was not totally divorced from social processes; but it was not totally determined by them; and in the exchange of ideas what counted most was the nature of the ideas themselves and the manner in which they were brought to bear upon each other: content and communication mattered more than context.

The missionaries and those who sent them had probably not anticipated that influences would be mutual, or that the dialogue would be more varied than one of acceptance or rejection. In a new environment, new forms evolved; variations that could not have been expected in England. A prophet in Israel deals with the predictable; a prophet in the wilderness must live with the unexpected.

ABBREVIATIONS

To avoid repetition, the location of the most frequently quoted source is not given in the notes, so it should be assumed that where there is no indication to the contrary the material cited is to be found in the New Zealand section of the archives of the Methodist Missionary Society, London, and unless indicated to the contrary was originally addressed to the Secretary of the Wesleyan Methodist Missionary Society. This material took three forms: letters, letters including journal extracts of varying dates, or journal extracts without any accompanying letter. Some of these items are now in other libraries, such as the Mitchell Library, Sydney, and in such cases this is indicated. Records listed as kept in Trinity Theological College are soon to be housed in the United College of St John the Evangelist, Auckland 5.

ADB:	Australian Dictionary of Biography.
AML:	Auckland Institute and Museum Library.
ANL:	Australian National Library, Canberra.
APL:	Auckland Public Library.
ATL:	Alexander Turnbull Library, Wellington.
CMS:	Church Missionary Society.
DNB:	Dictionary of National Biography.
DNZB:	Dictionary of New Zealand Biography.
HL:	Hocken Library, Dunedin.
HRNZ:	Historical Records of New Zealand.
JPS:	Journal of the Polynesian Society.
ML:	Mitchell Library, Sydney.
MMS:	Methodist Missionary Society, London.
NA:	National Archives, Wellington.
TTC:	Trinity Theological College, Auckland.
Uncat. MSS.:	Uncatalogued Manuscripts, Set 197, Item 1, Methodist Church Papers, Record of the Wesleyan Mission to New Zealand, 1823-7 (in the Mitchell Library, Sydney).
WMS:	Wesleyan Methodist Missionary Society.

NOTES

I: ORIGINS

1. 'Instructions of the Committee of the Wesleyan Methodist Missionary Society to Mr Leigh and Mr Morgan . . . read to them at a public ordination service in the New Chapel, City Road January 17 1821', Wesleyan Missionary Letters, 1823-64, ATL; copy also in the Hobbs Papers, TTC.
2. E. W. Hames, 'Walter Lawry and the Wesleyan Mission in the South Seas', *Wesley Historical Society (New Zealand) Proceedings,* Vol. 23, No. 4 (September 1967), p. 8.
3. Alexander Strachan, *Remarkable Incidents in the Life of the Rev. Samuel Leigh* (London, 1853), pp. 21-30.
4. Ibid., p. 32.
5. *ADB,* Vol. II, p. 105.
6. Strachan, p. 96.
7. J. R. Elder, *Marsden's Lieutenants* (Dunedin, 1934), p. 240n.
8. G. G. Findlay and W. W. Holdsworth, *The History of the Wesleyan Methodist Missionary Society* (London, 1921), Vol. III, p. 21.
9. Strachan, pp. 96-97.
10. Quoted in Hames, p. 7.
11. Ibid., p. 8.
12. Findlay and Holdsworth, p. 31.
13. W. Lawry, Parramatta, N.S.W., 6 October 1821, Transcript in J. A. Ferguson, W.M.S. Records, 1819-26, ANL.
14. Hames, p. 8.
15. Lawry, 6 October 1821, op. cit.
16. Ibid. While Lawry's strictures are to some extent suspect, Leigh had many other critics; and a detached appraisal of these conflicting versions of his career is long overdue.
17. For fuller details, see Findlay and Holdsworth, Vol. III, pp. 37-40.
18. William Hall's Journal in Elder, *Marsden's Lieutenants,* p. 220. The *Active* reached Sydney on 30 July 1819—*Sydney Gazette,* 31 July 1819.
19. Elder, *Marsden's Lieutenants,* p. 220.

20. John King, Letters and Journals, 1819-1853, 17 May-13 June 1819, HL.
21. For example, William Hall, 15 November 1819, and Thomas Kendall, 8 November 1819, with a copy of 'The New Zealanders' First Prayers', both to Leigh, MMS.
22. Strachan, pp. 102-3.
23. John King, 4 June 1819, op. cit.
24. Strachan, pp. 116-21. If the tent was the one used in New Zealand, it leaked.
25. Ibid., p. 122.
26. Findlay and Holdsworth, Vol. III, p. 172.
27. 'Gross annual expenditure of the Wesleyan Missionary Society on account of New Zealand since the commencement of the mission', N.Z. II 1835-40, MMS. By 1847 the Society had spent more than £80,000 on the mission.
28. Elder, *Marsden's Lieutenants,* pp. 163-6.
29. Published 1820. See Elder, *Marsden's Lieutenants,* p. 171 for a brief note on Lee.
30. Elder, *Marsden's Lieutenants,* p. 268. See also Andrew Sharp, *Crisis at Kerikeri* (Wellington, 1958), p. 63.
31. Diary of Rev. Walter Lawry, 1818-25, ML, recording a conversation Lawry had with Kendall.
32. Strachan, p. 124.
33. Elder, *Marsden's Lieutenants,* p. 171, n. 15.
34. Findlay and Holdsworth, Vol. III, p. 34; *Missionary Register* (February 1822), p. 94.
35. Strachan, p. 130. Mrs Catherine Leigh died at Parramatta, 15 May 1831, and Leigh later remarried, in August 1842.
36. Diary of Rev. Walter Lawry, 17 September 1821, ML.
37. Findlay and Holdsworth, Vol. III, p. 173.
38. *New Zealand Herald,* 26 November 1875; William White, Sydney, 29 January 1823, Australia I, 1812-26, MMS.
39. William White, Letter on Mission Work, 21 September 1824, ATL.
40. See J. G. Turner, *The Pioneer Missionary: Life of the Rev. Nathaniel Turner* (London, 1872), which is based on The Personal Narrative of Nathaniel Turner, 2 vols, ML.
41. Ibid., Vol. I, p. 9.
42. Elder, *Marsden's Lieutenants,* p. 225, and *Missionary Register* (August 1822), pp. 350-1.
43. Richard Watson also complained of his 'capriciousness'—Findlay and Holdsworth, Vol. III, p. 181.
44. These details are from Turner's Personal Narrative, Vol. I, and J. G. Turner, *The Pioneer Missionary. . . .* See also William White, At Sea, 31 March 1822.

45. Findlay and Holdsworth, Vol. III, p. 35.
46. G. Erskine, Sydney, 20 January 1823, Australia I, 1812-26, MMS.
47. William White, Sydney, 29 January 1823, Australia I, 1812-26, MMS.
48. B. Carvosso, Windsor, N.S.W., 15 July 1822, in R. McNab, ed., *Historical Records of New Zealand* (Wellington, 1908), Vol. 1, pp. 582-3.
49. These details are from J. Stack, Holborn Bridge, 3 December 1832—Secretary, CMS, Microfilmed archives of the Church Missionary Society, London, Reel 67, C.H./057, ATL. Wade appears to have joined Leigh at the same time as Stack—Journal of William Hall, 15 May 1823 in Elder, *Marsden's Lieutenants,* p. 228.
50. John Hobbs-WMS, 28 June 1824, Typescript ATL.
51. Hobbs's Journal, 22 February 1824, TTC.
52. John Hobbs, 28 June 1824, op. cit.
53. Ibid.
54. W. Moister, *Missionary Worthies* (London, 1885), pp. 404-5.
55. Minutes of meeting held Sydney, 30 June 1823, Transcript in J. A. Ferguson, W.M.S. Records, 1819-26, ANL.
56. Ibid., 10 July 1823.
57. William Hall's Journal, 15 May 1823, in Elder, *Marsden's Lieutenants,* p. 228.
58. For details see Judith Binney, *The Legacy of Guilt, A Life of Thomas Kendall* (Auckland, 1968), pp. 93-96, 101, 108; also Leigh-Marsden, 4 April 1822, in Rev. S. Marsden, Correspondence and Letters, 1819-38, Vol. IV, HL.
59. R. J. Barton, *Earliest New Zealand* (Masterton, 1927), pp. 226, 245, 255-6. Barton edited material, mainly from the Hocken Library, with a heavy hand, defending Butler's reputation against Marsden.
60. *Missionary Notices* (May 1822), p. 258.
61. Samuel Leigh-WMS, 25 February 1822, Uncat. MSS., ML. A more lurid version is in Strachan, pp. 183-7. See also S. Percy Smith, *Maori Wars of the Nineteenth Century* (Christchurch, 1910), pp. 181-90 and J. R. Elder, ed., *The Letters and Journals of Samuel Marsden, 1765-1838* (Dunedin, 1932), pp. 355-9.
62. Leigh-Marsden, 4 April 1822, op. cit.
63. Samuel Leigh-WMS, 27 February 1822, Uncat. MSS., ML. 'Ma-du' is presumably *maru,* which has many meanings, and 'crack hear', *karakia,* a charm, spell, or incantation, which is presumably how the Maoris interpreted Leigh's strange repetition of letters and words.
64. Strachan, p. 164.

65. Strachan, pp. 164, 174; Findlay and Holdsworth, Vol. III, p. 176; A. H. McLintock, ed., *An Encyclopaedia of New Zealand* (Wellington, 1966), Vol. II, p. 299.

66. Walter Lawry, Ship St. Michael, N.Z., to his parents in Cornwall, 25 July 1822, ATL; Personal Narrative of N. Turner, Vol. I, pp. 50-51, ML. See also White and Turner, 2 April 1824.

67. Extracts from Leigh's Journal, 27 April 1823, MMS. See also Barton, pp. 271-2; Elder, *L. and J. of Samuel Marsden*, pp. 359-61; and John King's Journal, 3 May 1823, in Elder, *Marsden's Lieutenants*, p. 255.

68. Diary of Rev. Walter Lawry, 1818-25, Typescript, ML.

69. E. W. Hames, 'Walter Lawry . . .', pp. 13-14. See also Lawry's diary, 4 January 1822.

70. W. Lawry, Parramatta, N.S.W., 6 October 1821, Transcript in J. A. Ferguson, W.M.S. Records, 1819-26, ANL. Lawry's colleagues, Mansfield and Walker, also made charges in a letter to the WMS committee of 19 October 1821 and Leigh defended himself against the charge of breach of promise in a letter to the WMS committee of 26 November 1821, Uncat. MSS, ML.

71. Lawry, Diary, 12 July 1822.

72. Ibid, 13 July 1822. Samuel Butler, later drowned in the Hokianga, was son of the Rev. John Butler and one of the reasons for Marsden's clash with them. For John Cowell, see Binney, *Legacy of Guilt,* and *DNZB,* Vol. I, pp. 178-9.

73. Lawry, Diary, op. cit., 15 July 1822. 'Kerra Kerra' was presumably chief Korokoro, who died in 1823—Elder, *L. and J. of Samuel Marsden,* p. 145n.

74. W. Lawry, Ship St. Michael, N.Z.-Rev. Josh. Taylor, WMS, London, 25 July 1822, quoted in Lawry's Diary.

75. Ibid. See also W. Lawry, Ship St. Michael, N.Z.-His father and mother in Cornwall, 25 July 1822, ATL.

76. Samuel Leigh, 16 November 1822, MMS; Strachan, p. 172, and Findlay and Holdsworth, Vol. III, p. 176, assert it was the ship's officers who traded in guns and powder. There does not appear to be any independent confirmation of Leigh's charges.

77. Findlay and Holdsworth, Vol. III, p. 176.

78. Strachan, pp. 165-8.

79. Elder, *Marsden's Lieutenants,* pp. 132, 220.

80. Samuel Leigh, 25 June 1823-WMS, Uncat. MSS, ML. The actual portrait is dated 1823.

81. Rev. J. Butler, Letters and Journals 1819-24, 31 March, 2 April 1823, HL; quoted in Barton, pp. 267-8. See also Leigh's version in loose pages of journal, much corrected, headed 1 March 1823; and also Strachan, pp. 168-70.

82. Strachan, p. 170.

83. Ibid.

II: EARLY DAYS AT WHANGAROA

1. White reported they arrived at midnight on the 15th, but he went ashore the next day. See White's Journal, 16 May 1823, TTC; William White, 24 May 1823; Barton, p. 273.
2. White's Journal, loc. cit.
3. Ibid.
4. King, a shoemaker, and Hall, a carpenter, had been catechists at Rangihoua since 1814; Kemp was a smith, acting as store-keeper at Kerikeri. Shepherd, also at Kerikeri, although having no trade, was a skilled gardener. See Elder, *L. and J. of Samuel Marsden,* p. 445.
5. William White, 24 May 1823, op. cit.
6. Barton, p. 274.
7. Samuel Leigh-Rev. J. Butler, 22 May 1823, Rev. J. Butler, Letters and Journals 1819-24, No. 25, HL; see also Barton, p. 273.
8. Barton, p. 274.
9. William White, 4 November 1823.
10. Barton, p. 276.
11. William White, Journal, 28 May 1823, TTC. In this phase of first horrified reaction, White referred to New Zealand as 'this Dark benighted land of Blood'—William White, 4 November 1823.
12. William White, Journal, 2 June 1823, TTC; Samuel Leigh, 5 June 1823.
13. William White, Journal, loc. cit.
14. Ibid., 3 June 1823.
15. Samuel Leigh, 5 June 1823.
16. Barton, p. 278. See also Sir Frederick R. Chapman, ed., *Journal Kept in New Zealand in 1820 by Ensign Alexander McCrae* (Wellington, 1928), p. 27, and Leslie G. Kelly, 'Some New Information Concerning the Ship Boyd', *JPS,* Vol. 49, No. 196 (December 1940), p. 600; Elder, *L. and J. of Samuel Marsden,* p. 430. There are so many variant spellings of Maori personal and tribal names in missionary writings of this period, that it is frequently difficult to identify individuals or to be certain how they should be rendered today. Te Pere, for example, should possibly be given as Te Pare.
17. S. Percy Smith, 'The Peopling of the North', *JPS,* Vol. 6 (1897), suplement, p. 13; R. McNab, *From Tasman to Marsden* (Dunedin, 1914), p. 136. Leslie G. Kelly, *Marion Dufresne at the Bay of Islands* (Wellington, 1951), pp. 99-100; J. S. Polack, *Manners and Customs of the New Zealanders* (London, 1840), Vol. II, p. 137. See also *New Zealand 1826-1827 from the French of Dumont D'Urville,* transl. Olive Wright (Wellington, 1950), p. 179.

18. William Williams, *Christianity among the New Zealanders* (London, 1867), p. 70.

19. S. Percy Smith, *Maori Wars of the Nineteenth Century* (Christchurch, 1910), p. 398. Yet on p. 349 he refers to Te Puhi as the leader of 'Ngati-Pou'.

20. Richard A. Cruise, *Journal of a Ten Months Residence in New Zealand (1820)*, ed. A. G. Bagnall (Christchurch, 1957), pp. 66-67.

21. Ibid., p. 66.

22. McNab, *From Tasman to Marsden*, pp. 114-5; Peter Dillon, *Narrative and Successful Result of a Voyage in the South Seas* (London, 1821), Vol. I, pp. 215-6.

23. Ibid., pp. 213-5.

24. 'The Deposition of John Besant relative to the Loss of the Boyd', sworn before Samuel Marsden, Justice of the Peace, 10 November 1813, in *HRNZ*, Vol. I, pp. 421-2.

25. McNab, *From Tasman to Marsden*, p. 117; *Sydney Gazette*, 17 July 1808; see also Dillon, loc. cit.

26. Alexander Berry, *Reminiscences of* . . . (Sydney, 1912), p. 54; McNab, *From Tasman to Marsden*, p. 118.

27. Journal of William Williams, 27 November 1832, Typescript, Vol. II, AML; *Church Missionary Record* (November 1833).

28. Hugh Carleton, *The Life of Henry Williams* (Auckland, 1874), Vol. I, p. 25n.

29. Open letter dictated by George, Wesleydale, Whangaroa, 6 November 1823, The Brisbane Documents, Series 12-17, Box IV, Ms. 4036, NK 787, ANL.

30. Elder, *L. and J. of Samuel Marsden*, p. 349. See also pp. 61-62, 85-89.

31. Jnl extract, 12 July 1823, in William White, 2 April 1824.

32. Cruise, pp. 19, 66-8, 114; Elder, *L. and J. of Samuel Marsden*, pp. 238, 250-1. See also *HRNZ*, Vol. I, pp. 485-7, 493-4.

33. *HRNZ*, Vol. I, pp. 551-2.

34. Cruise, p. 195.

35. *HRNZ*, Vol. I, p. 551.

36. Cruise, p. 168.

37. Ibid., pp. 165-7, 173.

38. *HRNZ*, Vol. I, p. 554.

39. Jnl extract, 12 February 1826, in J. Stack, 21 March 1826.

40. *HRNZ*, Vol. I, p. 496.

41. Cruise, p. 115.

42. Ibid., pp. 176-7. See also 'Journal of Proceedings of His Majesty's Colonial Cutter Mermaid from the 8th Day of May to the 15th Day of August 1823 inclusive, Kept by John Rodolphus Kent, Commander', Photoprint, A4037, ML.

43. *HRNZ*, Vol. I, p. 496. Cruise also noted examples of treachery, e.g., Cruise, pp. 190-1. See also J. L. Nicholas, *Narrative of a*

Voyage to New Zealand (London, 1817), Vol. II, pp. 136-7, which describes the 'lurking treachery' of George.

44. Cruise, pp. 190-3.
45. William White, Journal, 4-7 June 1823, TTC; Jnl extracts, 4-7 June 1823, in William White, 4 November 1823. The extracts differ slightly from the journal. See also Samuel Leigh, 5 June 1823, Uncat. MSS., ML.
46. Leigh's text was I Samuel, vii. 12: 'Then Samuel took a stone, and set it between Mizpeh and Shen, and called the name thereof Eben-ezer, saying, Hitherto hath the Lord helped us.'— Strachan, p. 179, Barton, p. 278; William White, Journal, 8 June 1823, TTC.
47. Ibid., 10 June 1823.
48. Leigh, 25 June 1823, Uncat. MSS., ML; Strachan, p. 201.
49. William White, Journal, 14 June 1823, TTC; Jnl extract, 25 June, in William White, 4 November 1823.
50. Barton, p. 280; Jnl extract, 24 June 1823, in William White, 4 November 1823.
51. Barton, p. 279; for original, see Rev. J. Butler, Letters and Journals 1819-24, No. 26, HL.
52. William White, Jnl extracts, op. cit., and his Journal, 10 July 1823, TTC. At this point White refers to 'strong temptation' and subsequent pages appear to have been torn out of his Journal.
53. Personal Narrative of Nathaniel Turner, Vol. I, pp. 52-53, ML.
54. William White, Journal, 6-7 July 1823. Turner describes Wade as 'by profession a sail-maker'—Personal Narrative of Nathaniel Turner, Vol. I, p. 51, ML.
55. J. Shepherd-Rev. J. Butler, Whangaroa, 4 August 1823, Rev. J. Butler, Letters and Journals, 1819-24, No. 30, HL. See also Barton, pp. 288-91.
56. The copy of Strachan in Massey University Library has many pencil annotations by a former owner to the effect that he heard Leigh describe such incidents. Strachan also states in his preface that he had many interviews with Leigh in the last year of his life.
57. Strachan, pp. 178 ff.
58. Samuel Leigh, 20 July 1823, Uncat. MSS., ML.
59. Jnl extract, 5 August 1823, in William White, 2 April 1824.
60. Elder, *L. and J. of Samuel Marsden*, p. 339.
61. Hobbs's Journal, 6 October-1 November 1823, TTC.
62. Jnl extract, 5 August 1823, in William White, 2 April 1824.
63. Elder, *L. and J. of Samuel Marsden*, p. 345.
64. Samuel Marsden-Joseph Butterworth, M.P., 22 December 1817, J. A. Ferguson, W.M.S. Typescripts and MSS, New Zealand 1823-7, ANL; see also Marsden-Butterworth, 21 July 1821, Australia I, 1812-26, MMS, also in *HRNZ*, Vol. I, pp. 563-5.

65. Elder, *L. and J. of Samuel Marsden,* p. 343.
66. Ibid., p. 348.
67. Personal Narrative of Nathaniel Turner, Vol. I, pp. 50-51, ML.
68. William White and Nathaniel Turner-WMS, 2 April 1824, in *HRNZ,* Vol. I, p. 625. For further criticism of Leigh, see Hobbs's Journal, 16 August 1828, TTC.
69 W. Lawry, Parramatta, 26 January 1824, Australia I, 1812-26, MMS.
70. Minutes . . . in ibid.
71. William Walker, 13 March 1824, Australia I, 1812-26, MMS.
72. William Walker, 26 January 1824, in ibid.
73. Robert Howe, 20 February 1824, Australia I, 1812-26, MMS.
74. Quoted in Findlay and Holdsworth, Vol. III, p. 46.
75. Samuel Marsden-Joseph Butterworth, M.P., 29 January 1824, Australia I, 1812-26, MMS; also in *HRNZ,* Vol. I, pp. 618-9.
76. Certificate of William Bland, surgeon, Sydney, 4 February 1824, enclosed with George Erskine-Rev. R. Watson, Sydney, 13 February 1824, Bonwick Transcripts, Missionary, Vol. 5, p. 1389, ML, which is also in *HRNZ,* Vol. I, p. 622. Leigh died in 1852 at the age of 66.
77. Old Land Claim No. 938, National Archives; quoted in R. A. A. Sherrin and J. H. Wallace, *Early History of New Zealand* (Auckland, 1890), pp. 272-3.
78. Personal Narrative of Nathaniel Turner, Vol. I, pp. 52-53, ML.
79. Hobbs's Journal, 6 October 1823, TTC.
80. Samuel Leigh-WMS, 18 August 1823, Uncat. MSS., ML.
81. Elder, *L. and J. of Samuel Marsden,* p. 348.
82. Nathaniel Turner-Geo Turner, Whangaroa, 11 August 1823, copy in Personal Narrative of Nathaniel Turner, Vol. II, ML.

III: THE DEATH OF GEORGE

1. N. Turner-WMS, 28 October 1823, Uncat. MSS., ML; Elder, *L. and J. of Samuel Marsden,* pp. 339, 365-370.
2. Ibid., p. 405; John King, Letters and Journals, 1819-23, 14 November 1823, HL. A few days earlier, on 6 November, George had dictated his letter about the *Boyd* affair, quoted earlier. At this stage he feared the Bay of Islands chiefs were coming to take the missionaries away and talked of going to Port Jackson himself.—Leigh, White and Turner-Marsden, 7 October 1823, Marsden Papers, pp. 87-89, ML.
3. Jnl extract, 8 November 1823, in Nathaniel Turner, 6 January 1824.
4. Hobbs's Journal, 23 December 1823, TTC.
5. Jnl extract, 7 November 1823, in Nathaniel Turner-WMS, 1 November 1823, Uncat. MSS., ML.

6. Hobbs's Journal, 24 November 1823, TTC. The building is described in Personal Narrative of Nathaniel Turner, Vol. I, pp. 52-53, ML.

7. Jnl extract, 4 December 1823, in Nathaniel Turner, 29 January 1824.

8. Hobbs's Journal, 1, 10, 11, 24-6 November, 26-7 December 1823, TTC.

9. Ibid., 15 December 1823.

10. Ibid., 25 December 1823.

11. Ibid., 19 January 1824.

12. Ibid., 22 February 1824.

13. William White, Sydney, N.S.W., 29 January 1824, Australia I, 1812-26, MMS.

14. William Walker, Parramatta, N.S.W., 26 January 1824, ibid.

15. Copy of Daniel Tyerman-Nathaniel Turner and William White, Sydney, 7 September 1824, N.Z.I., 1819-34, MMS.

16. White's Journal, 1-5 April 1824, TTC.

17. Ibid., 20 June 1824.

18. Ibid., 30 March, 6 May 1824.

19. Ibid., 27 June 1824.

20. Ibid., 7, 8, 12 August, 20-27 September 1824.

21. Ibid., 6 September 1824.

22. Jnl extract, 4 July 1824, in William White, 24 November 1824.

23. White's Journal, 15 June 1824, TTC.

24. Hobbs's Journal, 17 June 1824, TTC.

25. White's Journal, 19 June 1824, TTC. Later in the year, in sending Luke home to fetch his wife, White and Turner reported: 'During the last 4 months he has manifested a sincere desire to save his soul, has regularly met in class and been very diligent in all the means of grace'.—William White and Nathaniel Turner, 1 December 1824.

26. Hobbs's Journal, 7 January 1824, TTC.

27. Ibid., 5 June 1824.

28. Ibid., 21 February 1824.

29. Ibid., 23 February 1824.

30. Ibid., 13 April, 4 July 1824. After his dream, recorded on 4 July, in which 'my most beloved Mrs G . . . manifested all that was consistent with pure affection but did not seem willing to enter into the marriage state', Hobbs went on to dream that as a reward for this disappointment he was called to preach the Gospel in several of the South Sea Islands. Hobbs's dreams were often accurate prognostications, as in this case.

31. Ibid., 3 July 1824.

32. Ibid., 16 August 1824.

33. William White and Nathaniel Turner, 2 April 1824.

34. Nathaniel Turner-WMS, 30 June 1824, Uncat. MSS., ML.

35. Nathaniel Turner-Rev. J. Etchells, Bramley, 30 September 1824.

36. William White and Nathaniel Turner, 1 December 1824.
37. Hobbs's Journal, 30 December 1824, TTC; William White and Nathaniel Turner, 31 December 1824.
38. It is difficult to be certain of the correct spelling of 'Udi Whare', as it is variously rendered: 'Hoodoowarry', 'Hude', 'E'Udi', 'Ahoode', etc. His village was probably at Toropapa—Jnl extract, 12 June 1824, in William White, 24 November 1824.
39. White's Journal, 17, 18 March 1824, TTC.
40. Jnl extract, 12 June 1824, in William White, 24 November 1824.
41. Jnl extract, 5 May 1824, in Nathaniel Turner-WMS, 30 June 1824, Uncat. MSS., ML.
42. White's Journal, 4 May 1824, TTC.
43. William White and Nathaniel Turner-WMS, 30 June 1824, Uncat. MSS., ML. See also Jnl extract, 13 June, in Nathaniel Turner-WMS, 8 July 1824, Uncat. MSS., ML.
44. White and Turner, 30 June 1824, op. cit.
45. Jnl extracts, 20, 22 September 1824, in N. Turner, 23 November 1824.
46. White's Journal, 21 March 1824, TTC.
47. For example Hobbs's Journal, 18 July 1824, TTC.
48. Ibid., 29 August 1824.
49. Missionary references to 'Udi Whare', in all the variant spellings listed in footnote 38, may relate to Ngahuruhuru. Turner, for example, refers to 'Ahoode-Warre' as 'one of the most mild and civil men we have met with since we have been in New Zealand'—Jnl extract, 17 March 1824, in Nathaniel Turner-WMS, 18 June 1824, Uncat. MSS., ML. This accords with Cruise's description of Ngahuruhuru (which he spelt E hoodoo) —Cruise, p. 176.
50. White's Journal, 11 July 1824, TTC. See also Jnl extract for that date in William White, 24 November 1824; and White's Journal, 6 December 1824, TTC. His Journal of 22 November 1824 refers to being received at 'Ewai te Whare' by Kearoa's tribe.
51. White's Journal, 7 May 1824, TTC.
52. Ibid., 29 September 1824.
53. Ibid., 15 August 1824; Hobbs's Journal, 5 September 1824, TTC.
54. Jnl extract, 31 January 1824, in Nathaniel Turner, 30 January 1824.
55. White's Journal, 6 September 1824, TTC.
56. Hobbs's Journal, 18 January 1824, TTC.
57. White's Journal, 21 March 1824, TTC. There are many other references to dirt and lice, for example, William White, Letter on Mission Work, 21 September 1824, ATL.

58. White's Journal, 4 April 1824, TTC.
59. Jnl extract, 19 September 1824, in William White, 3 October 1824.
60. White's Journal, 14-15 November, 2, 13 December 1824, TTC.
61. Ibid., 20 November 1824. See also 15 November 1824.
62. Ibid., 27 October 1824.
63. Ibid., 2-4 November 1824; Hobbs's Journal, 2-5 November 1824, TTC.
64. Hobbs's Journal, 23-6 February, 11 March, 1 April, 21-29 May, 21-22 June, 19-31 July, 4-5 August 1824, TTC.
65. William White, Letter on Mission Work, 21 September 1824, ATL.
66. Ibid. See also Nathaniel Turner-Rev. J. Etchells, Bramley, 30 September 1824, MMS.
67. Ibid.: Hobbs's Journal, 19 January 1824, TTC; White's Journal, 1 May, 8 September 1824, TTC; and for comment on the state of mission premises in December, see John Beveridge, Ship St. Michael at Sea, 4 January 1825, Friendly Islands I, MMS.
68. Hobbs's Journal, ? February 1824, TTC.
69. White's Journal, 9 May 1824, TTC.
70. Ibid., 9 September 1824; Hobbs's Journal, 30 June 1824, TTC.
71. William White, Letter on Mission Work, 21 September 1824, ATL.
72. Marsden sent Michael Stack to help with the CMS mission. Henry Williams later commented that though a pious young man he was very different from his brother—'he is about as much use as the fifth wheel to a coach. . . .' Henry Williams-Samuel Marsden, 24 March, 2 August 1824, Samuel Marsden Papers, Vol. 3, New Zealand Missions 1816-1837, ML.
73. These details are from White, letter on Mission Work, op. cit.; Turner-Etchells, op. cit.; Jnl extract, 10 February 1824, in Nathaniel Turner-WMS, 17 June 1824, Uncat. MSS., ML; White's Journal, 8 September 1824, TTC.
74. Jnl extract, 29 March 1824, in Nathaniel Turner-WMS, 25 June 1824, Uncat. MSS., ML. There is also a reference in White's Journal, 27 February 1824, TTC, to 'Jackey' guarding several fine peach trees that he might give the fruit to the missionaries.
75. Jnl extract, 11 September 1824, in Nathaniel Turner, 23 November 1824.
76. References to shooting are in White's Journal, 26 February, 1 May, 10, 29 September, 27 October 1824, TTC; Jnl extracts, 9, 20 February 1824, in Nathaniel Turner-WMS, 17 June 1824, Uncat. MSS., ML.
77. Hobbs's Journal, 11, 26-28 March 1824; TTC; White's Journal, 28-29 March 1824, TTC.

78. Hobbs's Journal, 2-7 December 1824, TTC.

79. Ibid., 28 March 1824; White's Journal, 28 March 1824, TTC.

80. Henry Williams-Samuel Leigh, 2 April 1824, N.Z.I., 1819-34, MMS.

81. White's Journal, 6 July 1824, TTC.

82. Hobbs's Journal, 12 August 1824; White's Journal, 10-18 August 1824, TTC.

83. Ibid., 26 February 1824, TTC; Hobbs's Journal, 22-26 February 1824, TTC.

84. White's Journal, 15 July 1824; Jnl extracts, 15-16 July 1824, in William White, 24 November 1824; Jnl extract, 15 July 1824, in Nathaniel Turner, 23 November 1824; Hobbs's Journal, 16-17 July 1824, TTC; L. Threkeld-Samuel Leigh, Sydney, 29 September 1824, Australia I, 1812-24, MMS; James Montgomery (ed.), *Journal of Voyages and Travels, by Daniel Tyerman and George Bennet* . . . (London, 1831), Vol. II, pp. 127-40.

85. Hobbs's Journal, 14 October 1824, TTC; White's Journal, 13-18 October 1824, TTC. Captain Dacre was apparently looking for timber—Hobbs's Journal, 19-31 July 1824.

86. Ibid., 19 August, 30 December 1824.

87. White's Journal, 19 March 1824, TTC.

88. Hobbs's Journal, 13-30 December 1824, TTC.

89. Ibid., 20 May, 19, 30 December 1824; White's Journal, 8 September 1824, TTC.

90. Hobbs's Journal, 10-11 October 1824, TTC; White's Journal, 16 October 1824, TTC. For details of Tapsell, see for example, Elder, *L. and J. of Samuel Marsden,* pp. 553-4, Binney, *Legacy of Guilt,* pp. 111-2, n. 48; James Cowan, *A Trader in Cannibal Land, The Life and Adventures of Captain Tapsell* (Dunedin, 1935).

91. William White, 5 January 1825.

92. Later, when White wished to expand Wesleyan missionary activities southwards, he claimed that this visit to Thames and Waikato had this ultimate objective—Copy of William White-Henry Williams, 31 July 1834, N.Z.I., 1819-34, MMS.

93. William White, 5 January 1835.

94. Jnl extracts, 2 January, 1 February 1825, in Nathaniel Turner, 31 March 1825.

95. Jnl extract, 8 January 1825, in ibid.

96. James Stack, Jnl extract, 31 January 1825.

97. Jnl extract, 1 January 1825, in Nathaniel Turner, 31 March 1825.

98. Jnl extracts, 24-5 January 1825, in ibid.

99. Jnl extract, 11 February 1825, in ibid.

100. James Stack, Jnl extract, 7 January 1825.

101. Jnl extract, 8 January 1825, in Nathaniel Turner, 31 March 1825.
102. Jnl extract, 25 January 1825, in ibid.
103. James Stack, Jnl extracts, 30 January, 2, 6 February 1825.
104. Ibid., 5 February 1825.
105. Jnl extract, 9 January 1825, in Nathaniel Turner, 31 March 1825.
106. James Stack, Jnl extracts, 10, 30 January 1825.
107. Hobbs's Journal, 25 January 1825, TTC.
108. Jnl extracts, 31 January, 1 February 1825, in William White, 7 February 1825; John King, Letters and Journals, 1819-53, 1, 3 February 1825, HL.
109. Jnl extract, 2, 11 February 1825, in Nathaniel Turner, 31 March 1825; Hobbs's Journal, 20 February 1825, TTC. They do not appear to have attacked Ngatiuru, who were normally their allies.
110. Jnl extract, 3 February 1825, in William White, 7 February 1825.
111. Jnl extract, 5 February 1825, in Nathaniel Turner, 31 March 1825.
112. James Stack, Jnl extracts, 6-7 February 1825; Jnl extracts, 5-6 February 1825, in Nathaniel Turner, 31 March 1825. Julep is a sweet drink, calomel a laxative.
113. Ibid.
114. James Stack, Jnl extract, 9 February 1825.
115. Ibid., 12 February 1825.
116. Jnl extract, 4 March 1825, in Nathaniel Turner-WMS, 31 March 1825, Uncat. MSS., ML.
117. James Stack, Jnl extracts, 6 March 1825; Jnl extract, 5 March 1825, in Nathaniel Turner, 25 March 1825; Hobbs's Journal, 5 March 1825, TTC.
118. James Stack, Jnl extract, 6-9 March 1825; Hobbs's Journal, 6-7 March 1825, TTC. See also William White-WMS, 25 March 1825, Uncat. MSS., ML, for a vivid account of his adventures which shows the missionary as a more effective man of action than most of the ship's crew. However, Te Puhi later blamed the loss of the ship on the folly of those who took her out in a foul wind, despite a warning not to do so—Jnl extract, 3 March 1826, in James Stack-WMS, 12 October 1826, Uncat. MSS., ML.
119. James Stack, Jnl. extracts, 10, 12, 17, 20 March 1825.
120. Jnl extracts, 18 March 1825, in Nathaniel Turner, 25 March 1825.
121. John King, Letters and Journals, 1819-53, 20-24 March 1825, HL; also Jnl extract, 21 March 1825, in John Hobbs, 10 September 1825; James Stack, Jnl extracts, 21, 24 March 1825; Hobbs's Journal, 21, 24 March 1825, TTC.

122. Nathaniel Turner, 25 March 1825.

123. Jnl extract, 27 March 1825, in Nathaniel Turner-WMS, 31 March 1825, Uncat. MSS., ML.

124. James Stack, Jnl extracts, 26, 28 March 1825.

125. James Stack, Jnl extract, 28 March 1825. Stack does not identify this 'sister in law'; but it is probable that she was Te Puhi's wife, the importance of whose influence was gradually revealed later.

126. Ibid.

127. Hobbs's Journal, 27 March 1825, TTC; also Jnl extract, 27 March 1825, in John Hobbs, 10 September 1825.

128. Hobbs's Journal, 30 March 1825, TTC; Jnl extract, 30 March 1825, in John Hobbs, 10 September 1825; James Stack, Jnl extracts, 30, 31 March 1825.

129. James Stack, Jnl extract, 31 March 1825.

130. Hobbs's Journal, 1 April 1825, TTC; Jnl extract, 1 April 1825, in John Hobbs, 10 September 1825.

131. James Stack, Jnl extracts, 6-7 April 1825; Jnl extracts, 2, 5 April 1825, in John Hobbs, 10 September 1825.

132. Jnl extract, 8 April 1825, in Nathaniel Turner, 1 September 1825.

133. William White, 12 April 1825.

134. Hobbs's Journal, 17 April 1825, TTC.

135. Ibid.; James Stack, Jnl extract, 17 April 1825. Later they learnt there had been a debate whether to rob the missionaries, but that Ngahuruhuru and Te Puhi had opposed this—James Stack, Jnl extract, 23 June 1825.

136. James Stack, Jnl extract, 18 April 1825.

137. Hobbs's Journal, 18 April 1825, TTC; see also Stack, Jnl extract, 18 April 1825.

138. James Stack, Jnl extract, 19 April 1825; Jnl extracts, 18-19 April 1825, in Nathaniel Turner, 1 September 1825; Hobbs's Journal, 23 April 1825, TTC.

139. James Stack, Jnl extracts, 2, 7 May 1825.

140. Ibid., 5 May 1825; Jnl extract, 4 May 1825, in Nathaniel Turner, 1 September 1825.

141. Jnl extracts, 27 April, 7 May 1825, in ibid.

142. James Stack, Jnl extract, 24 April 1825.

143. Hobbs's Journal, 24-30 April 1825, TTC.

144. James Stack, Jnl extract, 12 May 1825.

145. Ibid., 7 May 1825.

146. Ibid., 12 May 1825.

147. Ibid., 23 May 1825.

148. Hobbs's Journal, 8 June 1825.

149. Jnl extracts, 22-7 June 1825, in Nathaniel Turner, 8 September 1825.

150. Ibid., 27 June 1825.
151. James Stack, Jnl extract, 28 June 1825.
152. William White, Nathaniel Turner, John Hobbs, 30 June 1825.

IV: 'DREADFUL DEPRAVITY'

1. Hobbs's Journal, 13 June 1825, TTC.
2. Ibid., 2 July 1825.
3. James Stack, Jnl extract, 11 July 1825.
4. Jnl extract, 13 July 1825, in Nathaniel Turner, 8 September 1825.
5. Jnl extract, 29 July 1825, in ibid.; James Stack, Jnl extract, 29 July 1825.
6. Hobbs's Journal, 17 June 1825, TTC.
7. Jnl extract, 17 July 1825, in Nathaniel Turner, 8 September 1825; James Stack, Jnl extract, 17 July 1825.
8. Jnl extract, 19, 20 July 1825, in Turner, op. cit.; James Stack, Jnl extract, 20 July 1825.
9. Tareha, a Ngapuhi chief of Ngatirehua, who lived at Kerikeri— see Lawrence M. Rogers, ed., *The Early Journals of Henry Williams* (Christchurch, 1961), p. 54n; Edward Markham, *New Zealand or Recollections of it,* ed. E. H. McCormick (Wellington, 1963), p. 103n, 162; Richard Taylor, *Te Ika A Maui* (London, 1870) pp. 517-9, J. S. Polack wrote of him in *New Zealand* (London, 1838), Vol. II, p. 274; 'Tarria is a monster in size, and the brutality of his tastes correspond. I have seen this man swallow the contents of a bucket, full of cook's dripping and slush, alongside a ship, and then request a second edition of the filthy mess. This ogre has nearly consumed *a baby at a meal,* without any after complaint or inconvenience and indigestion.'
10. Hongi's visit is described in Jnl extracts, 21-26 July 1825, in N. Turner, 8 September 1825; James Stack, Jnl extracts, 23-27 July 1825, and Hobbs's Journal, entered under 23-25 August in error for July 1825, TTC.
11. James Stack, Jnl extract, 12, 13 August 1825.
12. Ibid., 15 August 1825; Jnl extract, 15 August 1825, in Nathaniel Turner, 12 September 1825.
13. James Stack, Jnl extract, 16 August 1825.
14. Ibid., 25, 30 August 1825.
15. Jnl extract, 29 October 1825, in James Stack, 29 March 1826.
16. James Stack, Jnl extract, 27 August 1825.
17. Ibid., 26-27 August 1825.
18. Nathaniel Turner, 1 September 1825.
19. Jnl extracts, 13, 19, 22, 27, 28 July 1825, in Nathaniel Turner, 8 September 1825.
20. James Stack, Jnl extract, 9 August 1825.

21. Jnl extract, 13 August 1825, in Nathaniel Turner, 8 September 1825.
22. Jnl extract, 30 August 1825, in ibid., and 5 September 1825, in N. Turner, 12 September 1825.
23. Hobbs's Journal, 18 August 1825, TTC.
24. William White, Nathaniel Turner, and John Hobbs, 17 September 1825. Many items from their list have been omitted.
25. James Stack, Jnl extract, 30 August 1825.
26. Ibid., 8 August 1825.
27. Jnl extract, 25 August 1825, in Nathaniel Turner, 12 September 1825.
28. Ibid., 5 September 1825.
29. Jnl extract, 23 September 1825, in James Stack, 29 March 1826.
30. Quoted in Nathaniel Turner, 13 September 1825.
31. Ibid.
32. John Hobbs, 20 September 1825. The name is sometimes spelt Brogreff and sometimes Broggref.
33. Nathaniel Turner, 13 September 1825.
34. John Hobbs, 20 September 1825.
35. Hobbs's Journal, 21-28 September, entered under 3 October 1825, TTC.
36. Jnl extract, 29 September 1825, in Nathaniel Turner, 20 February 1826.
37. Ibid.
38. Turner and Hobbs, 27 December 1825.
39. Ibid. In October, Turner and Hobbs were studying English Grammars, reading Cobbett's 'System which is written in the form of letters to his son', between six and seven each evening —Hobbs's Journal, 10, 11 October 1825, TTC. See also Jnl extract, 15 October 1825, in James Stack, 29 March 1826.
40. Hobbs's Journal, 2 October 1825, TTC; Jnl extract, 16 October 1825, in John Hobbs, 21 March 1826.
41. Hobbs's Journal, 2 October 1825, TTC; Nathaniel Turner and John Hobbs, 27 December 1825.
42. Jnl extract, 1 October 1825, in James Stack, 29 March 1826.
43. Jnl extract, 4 December 1825, in Nathaniel Turner, 20 February 1826; see also, Jnl extract, 4 December 1825, in James Stack, 29 March 1826.
44. Jnl extract, 30 November 1825, in James Stack, 29 March 1826.
45. Jnl extract, 8 November 1825, in ibid. See also ibid., 2 December 1825.
46. Jnl extract, 9 November 1825, in James Stack, 29 March 1826.
47. Jnl extract, 29 December 1825, in ibid.
48. Jnl extract, 6 November 1825, in Nathaniel Turner, 20 February 1826.
49. Jnl extract, 30 October 1825, in ibid.

50. Hobbs's Journal, 4 November 1825, **TTC**.
51. Jnl extract, 19 November 1825, in John Hobbs, 22 March 1826.
52. The events of these weeks are described in: Jnl extracts, 8-21, 31 December 1825, in Nathaniel Turner, 20 February 1826; Jnl extracts, 16-23 December 1825, in James Stack, 29 March 1826; Nathaniel Turner and John Hobbs, 27 December 1825; Hobbs's Journal, 19 December 1825, **TTC**.
53. He had apparently heard of Norfolk Island from Te Pahi, the Bay of Islands chief, who died in 1810, and who, he said, had cut his hair there and left it on the island as a *rahui,* or prohibition, against anyone else taking possession—Jnl extract, 6 December 1825, in James Stack, 29 March 1826.
54. Jnl extract, 12 October 1825, in ibid.
55. Jnl extract, 27 October 1825, in Nathaniel Turner, 20 February 1826; Jnl extract, 28-9 October 1825, in James Stack, 29 March 1826.
56. Jnl extract, 30 October 1825, in ibid.
57. Jnl extract, 29 October 1825, in ibid.; Jnl extract, 29 October, in John Hobbs, 21 March 1826.
58. Jnl extract, 6 November 1825, in James Stack, 29 March 1826.
59. Jnl extract, 19 November 1825, in John Hobbs, 22 March 1826.
60. White's Journal, 1 January-11 February 1826, **TTC**.
61. Hobbs's Journal, 13 February 1826, **TTC**.
62. White's Journal, 13 February 1826, **TTC**.
63. G. Morley, London-G. Erskine, Sydney, n.d., Wesleyan Mission Papers No. 1, Letters from W.M.S., London, 1823-8, MSS. Papers 66, ATL.
64. William White, London-John Hobbs, New Zealand, c/o R. Mansfield, New South Wales, n.d. This letter is at the front of White's Journal at TTC, and it is possible it was never sent.
65. Nathaniel Turner-WMS, 2 October 1826, Uncat. MSS., ML. See also, Nathaniel Turner and James Stack-R. Mansfield, Sydney, 3 October 1826, Wesleyan Missionary Letters, 1823-64, ATL.
66. Jnl extract, 22 February 1826, in John Hobbs, 25 March 1826. The phrase 'howling wilderness' is probably an echo of Deuteronomy 32:10.

V: THE SACK OF WHANGAROA

1. Jnl extract, 5 January 1826 in Nathaniel Turner, 20 February 1826. The passage is bracketed in different coloured ink, with a question mark.
2. Jnl extract, 13 April 1826, in James Stack, 12 October 1826.
3. Jnl extract, 5 February 1826, in Nathaniel Turner, 20 February 1826.

4. Jnl extracts, 14-20 April 1826, in James Stack, 12 October 1826; Jnl extracts, 16-20 April 1826, in John Hobbs, 10 November 1826; Personal Narrative of Nathaniel Turner, Vol. 1, p. 127, ML; Hobbs's Journal, 16-20 April 1826, TTC. Hobbs called the child Nathaniel; Turner's Personal Narrative, written many years later, called him Charles Bailey. In his journal, Hobbs recorded spending a fortnight making a mock iron fence for the grave, which Turner thought might cause him to be criticized, it was so ornate. So Hobbs spent another week putting up a plainer one.

5. Jnl extract, 25 June 1826, in James Stack-WMS, Uncat. MSS., ML.

6. Jnl extract, 25 November 1826, in Nathaniel Turner-WMS, 3 January 1827, Uncat. MSS., ML; for other brief references to Pakeha-Maoris, see Jnl extract, 26-27 November 1826, in James Stack-WMS, 17 January 1827, and Jnl extract, 29 August 1826, in James Stack-WMS, 12 October 1826, both Uncat. MSS., ML; and for previous year, James Stack, Jnl extract, 13 May 1825.

7. Jnl extract, 9 April 1826, in James Stack-WMS, 12 October 1826, Uncat. MSS., ML.

8. Jnl extract, 28 June 1826, in ibid.

9. Jnl extract, 10 September 1826, in James Stack-WMS, 12 October 1826, Uncat. MSS., ML.

10. Jnl extract, 31 December 1826, in James Stack-WMS, 17 January 1827, Uncat. MSS., ML.

11. Jnl extract, 4 December 1826, in James Stack-WMS, 17 January 1827; Jnl extract, 4 December 1827, in Nathaniel Turner-WMS, 3 January 1827, both in Uncat. MSS., ML.

12. Jnl extract, 10 January 1826, in Nathaniel Turner, 20 February 1826; Jnl extract, 21 January 1826, in James Stack, 29 March 1826.

13. Jnl extract, 28 August 1826, in James Stack-WMS, 12 October 1826, Uncat. MSS., ML.

14. Nathaniel Turner and James Stack-Rev. R. Mansfield, Mission House, Sydney, 3 October 1826, Wesleyan Missionary Letters 1823-64, ATL.

15. Jnl extract, 26 March 1826, in John Hobbs, 10 November 1826; John Hobbs, 3 April 1826; Hobbs's Journal, 5-6 April 1826, TTC.

16. Jnl extract, 28 October 1826, in John Hobbs, 30 November 1826; Jnl extract, 28 October 1826, in James Stack-WMS, 17 January 1827, Uncat. MSS., ML.

17. Nathaniel Turner and James Stack-Rev. R. Mansfield, Mission House, Sydney, 3 October 1826, Wesleyan Missionary Letters, 1823-64, ATL; Jnl extract, 30 November 1826, in James Stack-

WMS, 17 January 1827, Uncat. MSS., ML; Hobbs's Journal, 9 December 1826, TTC.

18. Jnl extract, 26 March 1826, in John Hobbs, 10 November 1826.
19. Nathaniel Turner-Rev. R. Mansfield, Sydney, 24 July 1826, Wesleyan Missionary Letters 1823-64, ATL.
20. Ibid.
21. Hobbs's Journal, 22 July 1826, TTC; Jnl extract, 16 July 1826, in John Hobbs, 10 November 1826.
22. Jnl extract, 21 January 1826, in James Stack, 29 March 1826; Hobbs's Journal, 22 February 1826, TTC.
23. The epidemic is described in Jnl extracts, 6-7, 9-10, 16, 18 December 1826, in James Stack-WMS, 17 January 1827, and Jnl extracts, 9-18 December 1826, in Nathaniel Turner-WMS, 3 January 1827, both Uncat. MSS., ML; William Williams's Journal, 19 December 1826, Typescript, AML.
24. Jnl extract, 5 March 1826, in James Stack-WMS, 12 October 1826, Uncat. MSS., ML.
25. Jnl extract, 27 April 1826, in ibid.
26. Jnl extract, 9 May 1826, in ibid.
27. Jnl extract, 18 May 1826, in ibid.
28. Jnl extract, 28 May 1826, in ibid.
29. Jnl extract, 1 July 1826, in ibid.; Hobbs's Journal, 15 July 1826, TTC, quoted in John Hobbs, 10 November 1826.
30. Jnl extract, 10 August 1826, in James Stack, op. cit., 12 October 1826.
31. Jnl extract, 17 October 1826, in James Stack-WMS, 17 January 1827, Uncat. MSS., ML.
32. Jnl extract, 23 June 1826, in James Stack-WMS, 12 October 1826, Uncat. MSS., ML.
33. Ibid
34. Jnl extract, 28 July 1826, in ibid.
35. Jnl extract, 13 September 1826, in ibid.
36. Jnl extract, 23 October 1826, in James Stack-WMS, 17 January 1827, Uncat. MSS., ML; see also 22 October 1826, ibid; Jnl extracts, 22-23 October 1826, in John Hobbs, 30 November 1826.
37. Jnl extract, 10 November 1826, James Stack, op. cit., 17 January 1827.
38. Jnl extract, 12 November 1826, in Nathaniel Turner-WMS, 3 January 1827, Uncat. MSS., ML.
39. Jnl extract, 15 (entered as 14) November 1826, in James Stack-WMS, 17 January 1827, Uncat. MSS., ML.
40. These details are based on Jnl extracts, 20-23 November 1826, in ibid.; Jnl extracts, 9-21 November 1826, in Nathaniel Turner-WMS, 3 January 1827, Uncat. MSS., ML; Hobbs's Journal, 20-21 November 1826, TTC.

41. Jnl extract, 25 November 1826 in James Stack-WMS, 17 January 1827. Uncat. MSS., ML.

42. Henry Williams, Paihia, 14 December 1826, Williams Papers, ATL.

43. See especially, George Clarke, Letters and Journals, 1822-49, Vol. I, Item 18, HL; Correspondence of James Kemp, APL; Jnl extracts, 17 November-7 December 1826, in James Stack-WMS, 17 January 1827, Uncat. MSS., ML.

44. Jnl extract, 6 December 1826, in James Stack, ibid.

45. Jnl extract, 16 November 1826, in ibid.

46. Jnl extract, 20 November 1826, in ibid.

47. Jnl extract, 5 December 1826, in ibid.

48. Jnl extract, 7 December 1826, in Nathaniel Turner-WMS, 3 January 1827, Uncat. MSS., ML.

49. Jnl extract, 20 December 1826, in ibid.

50. Hobbs's Journal, 20 December 1826, TTC.

51. Jnl extract, 20 December 1826, in Nathaniel Turner-WMS, 3 January 1827, Uncat. MSS., ML. The episode is also described in Jnl extract, 21 December 1826, in James Stack-WMS, 17 January 1827, Uncat. MSS., ML; William Williams's Journal, Vol. 1, 20 December 1826, Typescript, AML.

52. Jnl extract, 25 December 1826, in James Stack, op. cit., 17 January 1827; see also ibid., 22-24 December 1826.

53. Jnl extract, 30 December 1826, in ibid.

54. Jnl extract, 31 December 1826, in Nathaniel Turner, 3 January 1827, op. cit.

55. Hobbs's Journal, 31 December 1826, TTC.

56. Jnl extract, 31 December 1826, in Nathaniel Turner, 3 January 1827, op. cit.

57. Jnl extract, 3 December 1826, in ibid.; Hobbs's Journal, 3 December 1826, TTC.

58. George Clarke, Letters and Journals, 1822-1849, Vol. 1, 6 January 1827, HL.

59. Hobbs's Journal, 6 January 1827, TTC.

60. Jnl extract, 4 January 1827, in James Stack, 17 January 1827, op. cit.

61. Jnl extracts, 5-6 January 1827, in ibid.; Hobbs's Journal, 6 January 1827, TTC.

62. Stack, op. cit., 7 January 1827, says daughter; Hobbs, op. cit., 8 January 1827, says wife of Hongi.

63. Stack, op. cit., 8 January 1827; Hobbs, op. cit., 8 January 1827; Jnl extract, 9 January 1827, in Nathaniel Turner-WMS, 15 January 1827, Uncat. MSS., ML.

64. For details of this incident see Rogers, ed., *Early Journals of Henry Williams,* pp. 34-7; Augustus Earle, *Narrative of a Residence in New Zealand,* ed. E. H. McCormick (Oxford, 1966), pp. 31, 119-21; Sherrin and Wallace, pp. 328-34.

65. For these events, see Jnl extract, 9 January 1827, in Nathaniel Turner, 15 January 1827, op. cit.; Jnl extract, 9 January 1827, in James Stack, 17 January 1827, op. cit.; Hobbs's Journal, 9 January 1827, TTC; Personal Narrative of Nathaniel Turner, Vol. 1, pp. 143 ff., ML.

66. Jnl extract, 9 January 1827, in Nathaniel Turner, 15 January 1827, op. cit.

67. Jnl extracts, 9-10 January 1827, in James Stack, 17 January 1827, op. cit.

68. Jnl extract, 9 January 1827, in Nathaniel Turner, 15 January 1827, op. cit.

69. Hobbs's Journal, 10 January 1827, TTC; Jnl extract, 10 January 1827, in Nathaniel Turner, 15 January 1827, op. cit.

70. Hobbs, op. cit., 10 January 1827.

71. Turner, op. cit., 10 January 1827.

72. Ibid.

73. Ibid.

74. According to Turner's account; Hobbs's account gives more of the credit to Mrs Turner.

75. Te Wharenui or Te Wharerahi, was also the brother of Rewa of the Waimate—Hobbs, op. cit., 10 January 1827. He was one of a select category of Maoris who held the role, later often taken over by missionaries, of peacemaker—Earle, *Narrative,* pp. 126-7 n. 2.

76. Hobbs, op. cit., 10 January 1827.

77. Ibid. Turner's version was that 'Our poor old chief Te Puhi' came up to them 'with his heart apparently full to see us quitting his abode' and saying reassuringly in broken English, 'No more patu patu white man'—Turner, op. cit., 10 January 1827.

78. Turner wrote that they were told to stand near the water, Hobbs that they were ordered to kneel down close together 'which we did not knowing that we were ever to rise again'.

79. As well as Turner and Hobbs, op. cit., see *The Early Journals of Henry Williams,* pp. 36-37, and George Clarke, Letters and Journals 1822-1849, Vol. 1, 10 January 1827, HL.

80. Jnl extract, 11 January 1827, in James Stack-WMS, 17 January 1827, Uncat. MSS., ML; Hobbs's Journal, 11 January 1827, TTC.

81. Jnl extract, 11 January 1827, in Nathaniel Turner, op. cit., 15 January 1827.

82. Ibid., 12 January 1827; Hobbs's Journal, 11 January 1827, TTC. According to Percy Smith, *Maori Wars of the Nineteenth Century,* pp. 398-9, Hongi was shot by a 'young man connected with the Taou branch of Ngati-Whatua, named Maratea, but whose father was a Ngati-Pou' at a fight at Hunuhunua on the banks of the Mangamuka branch of the Hokianga river. Stack later referred to 'Maritea', then living at Pakanae, under

the protection of Moetara, as the man who shot Hongi—Jnl extract, 14 February 1830, in James Stack, 3 September 1830. See also, Sherrin and Wallace, p. 296.

83. Hobbs's Journal, 16 January 1827, TTC; James Kemp, Letters and Journals, 1819-57, 16 January 1827, HL; Jnl extract, 16 January 1827, in James Stack, 17 January 1827, op. cit.

84. Jnl extract, 16 January 1827, in Nathaniel Turner, 15 January 1827, op. cit. In this letter, Turner also paid tribute to Luke Wade: 'His conduct since he returned to us has been not only highly becoming but in many things praiseworthy. Poor man he lost his All in our general plunder.'

85. Henry Williams-Dandeson Coates, Sec. CMS, London, 17 January 1827, New Zealand C.N/O., Rev. H. Williams (a), Letters 1823-35, Micro. MSS., 222, ATL.

86. Hobbs's Journal, 17 January 1827, TTC.

87. George Clarke, Letters and Journals, 1822-49, Vol. 1, 17 January 1827, HL; Jnl extract, 18 January 1827, in James Stack, 17 January 1827, op. cit. For Tinana, see Binney, *Legacy of Guilt*, p. 23 n. 46.

88. Clarke, op. cit., 24 January 1827. See also, Jnl extract, 24 January 1827, in James Stack-WMS, 7 March 1827, Uncat. MSS., ML.

89. Hobbs's Journal, 19 January 1827, TTC.

90. Ibid., 18 January 1827.

91. Ibid., 19 January 1827.

92. Ibid., also Jnl extracts, 19-20 January 1827, in James Stack, 7 March 1827, op. cit.

93. Ibid., 22 January 1827.

94. Ibid., 23 January 1827.

95. Ibid., 24 January 1827.

96. Ibid., 27 January 1827.

97. Hobbs's Journal, 28 January 1827, TTC.

98. Jnl extracts, 27 January-9 February 1827, in James Stack, op. cit., 7 March 1827; Hobbs's Journal, 9 February 1827, TTC. According to Sherrin and Wallace, p. 333, the prisoners were tried at Port Jackson, and a number were hanged, the rest sentenced to work in irons for life on Norfolk Island.

VI: WHY WAS WHANGAROA ATTACKED?

1. Hobbs's Journal, 9 February 1827, TTC.

2. *Sydney Gazette*, 14 February 1827.

3. Minutes of a special District Meeting . . . Sydney, 15 February 1827, Wesleyan Missionary Letters, 1823-64, ATL.

4. *New Zealand Narrative by the Wesleyan Missionaries* (Sydney, R. Howe, Government Printer, 1827), Uncat. MSS., ML. See

also, *Church Missionary Register* (1827), p. 338 et. seq., and an edited version in Elder, *L. and J. of Samuel Marsden,* pp. 430-41; also John A. Ferguson, *Bibliography of Australia* (Sydney, 1941), Vol. 1, p. 420.

5. *Sydney Gazette,* 25 April 1827.
6. J. Orton, Journal, 1840-1, 26 February 1840, ML.
7. Hobbs's Journal, 18 March-25 July 1827, TTC. See also J. G. Turner, *The Pioneer Missionary,* pp. 79-80.
8. *Sydney Gazette,* 27 August 1827.
9. Strachan, p. 280.
10. Alfred Saunders, *History of New Zealand* (Christchurch, 1896), Vol. 1, pp. 90-91.
11. Extracts from George Clarke's Journal, 12 November 1826-6 August 1827, 24 January 1827, MSS. Vol. 60, HL.
12. Ibid., 13 December 1826.
13. Hugh Carleton, *Life of Henry Williams,* Vol. 1, p. 73, has the story that Pango, a leading chief from Rotorua, bewitched Hongi. See ibid., pp. 62-65 for an account of Hongi's career.
14. Hobbs's Journal, 13 January 1827, TTC.
15. Jnl extract, 17 January 1827, in James Stack-WMS, 17 January 1827, Uncat. MSS., ML.
16. William Williams's Journal, Vol. 1, 16 February 1827, Typescript, AML. William Pember Reeves, in *The Long White Cloud* (London, 1898), p. 153, thought the missionaries were plundered according to the law of *muru,* because they were Hongi's dependents and he had been wounded; but this interpretation hardly fits the facts.
17. Stack, op. cit., 17 January 1827.
18. Jnl extract, 9 January 1827, in Nathaniel Turner-WMS, 15 January 1827, Uncat. MSS., ML.
19. Quoted in Elder, *L. and J. of Samuel Marsden,* p. 434.
20. Findlay and Holdsworth, Vol. III, p. 193.
21. Hobbs's Journal, 10 January 1827, TTC.
22. Jnl extract, 8 January 1827, in J. Stack, op. cit., 17 January 1827.
23. Jnl extract, 22 January 1827, in James Stack-WMS, 7 March 1827, Uncat. MSS., ML.
24. William Williams's Journal, Vol. 1, 29 January 1827, Typescript, AML. In his published work, however, Williams followed the conventional line of attributing the sacking simply to Hongi's stragglers—Williams, *Christianity Among the New Zealanders,* p. 71.
25. Williams's Journal, op. cit., 16 February 1827.
26. George Clarke-CMS, 6 March 1827, George Clarke, Letters and Journals 1822-49, Vol. 1, Item 18, HL. As Clarke put it, Te Puhi, expecting that all advantages from the missionaries towards him had subsided, 'determined on making one general

plunder, to possess himself of their property and to keep others from enjoying any advantage from them'. As Clarke understood it, Hongi was the unintentional cause of trouble, for if he had not gone there, Te Puhi might not have decided to plunder the missionaries. See also Sherrin and Wallace, p. 286.

27. Jnl extract, 5 January 1827, in Stack, op. cit., 17 January 1827.
28. Jnl extract, 18 May 1826, in James Stack-WMS, 12 October 1826, Uncat. MSS., ML.
29. Jnl extract, 15 November 1827, in John Hobbs, n.d.
30. William Williams's Journal, Vol. 1, 5 February 1827, Type-script AML.
31. Hobbs's Journal, 19 January 1827, TTC; Jnl extract, 19 January 1827, in James Stack-WMS, 7 March 1827, Uncat. MSS., ML.
32. Jnl extract, 22 January 1827, in Stack, ibid. Patuone's desire not to be associated with the attack while at the same time benefiting from it, has some parallels with Hongi's approach to the situation.
33. Jnl extract, 8 January 1827, in Stack, op. cit., 17 January 1827.
34. James Stack, Jnl extract, 12 February 1825.
35. Jnl extract, 22 January 1827, in James Stack, op. cit., 7 March 1827. Hauhau was a famous *tohunga,* and his son was one of the mission boys taken to Tonga by Turner. Stack later said that Hauhau had been given the task of murdering the mis-sionaries by George—Jnl extract, 8 May 1829, in James Stack, 3 September 1830.
36. J. Orton, Journal, 1840-1, 26 February 1840, ML.
37. Quoted in J. G. Turner, *The Pioneer Missionary,* p. 77.
38. Jnl extract, 17 January 1827, in James Stack, 17 January 1827, op. cit.
39. William Williams's Journal, Vol. 1, 5 February 1827, Type-script, AML.

VII: THE SOCIAL CONTEXT OF MISSIONARY ACTIVITY

1. Harrison Wright, *New Zealand, 1769-1840: Early Years of Western Contact* (Cambridge, Massachusetts, 1959), p. 117.
2. Ibid., pp. 138-40.
3. Ibid., pp. 143-4.
4. Keith Sinclair, *A History of New Zealand* (Harmondsworth, 1969), pp. 38-39; Eric Schwimmer, *The World of the Maori* (Wellington, 1966), pp. 104-6.
5. Nathaniel Turner and John Hobbs, Trade Account for 1 July-31 December 1825, 11 February 1826.
6. Henry Williams-CMS, 31 March 1825, Micro. MSS. 227, Reel 65, ATL.

7. Hobbs's Journal, 2 April 1825, TTC. See also Jnl extracts, 2 April 1825, in John Hobbs, 10 September 1825.
8. James Stack, Jnl extract, 6 April 1825.
9. *The Collected Writings of Edward Irving* (London, 1864), Vol. 1, pp. 425-523. Irving's sermon, and the earlier missionary theory of James Douglas of Cavers, that Christianity should be propagated by colonizing and the introduction of the arts, are discussed in W. N. Gunson, *Evangelical Missionaries in the South Seas, 1797-1860,* Ph.D. thesis, Australian National University, 1959, pp. 102-3. Although Irving's name is not mentioned, Hobbs does refer to the text used by Irving.
10. Dillon, *Narrative and Successful Result . . .,* Vol. II, pp. 334-5.
11. Hobbs's Journal, 2 April 1825, TTC.
12. Arthur S. Thomson, *The Story of New Zealand, Past and Present—Savage and Civilized* (London, 1859), Vol. I, pp. 309-10.
13. The theory is applied to related situations in David Aberle, 'A Note on Relative Deprivation Theory as applied to Millenarian and other cult movements', in Sylvia L. Thrupp (ed.), *Millennial Dreams in Action; essays in Comparative Study* (Hague, 1962), pp. 209-14.
14. Jnl extract, 11 June 1826, in James Stack-WMS, 12 October 1826, Uncat. MSS., ML. On this occasion Te Puhi told Stack of a white man who came many years before, called Tai Maru, who was killed while landing from a boat. The anecdote, presumably a reference to Marion du Fresne, is perhaps indicative of repressed hostility to the missionaries, and of an attempt to bolster self esteem.
15. A. R. Radcliffe-Brown, 'Social Sanction', in *Encyclopaedia of the Social Sciences* (New York, 1934), Vol. 13, pp. 531-4. See also A. L. Epstein, 'Sanctions', in *International Encyclopedia of the Social Sciences* (New York, 1968), Vol. 14, pp. 1-5.
16. The concept of controlled violence is used by Binney, *Legacy of Guilt,* p. 79.
17. White's Journal, 6 May 1824, TTC.
18. Max Gluckman's analysis in 'The Peace in the Feud', *Past and Present,* 1955, No. 8, pp. 1-14, can be drawn on in this context.
19. Ralph Linton, 'Nativistic Movements', *American Anthropologist,* Vol. 45, 1943, pp. 230-40.

VIII: THE EXCHANGE OF IDEAS

1. On these themes, see two earlier articles: J. M. R. Owens, 'Christianity and the Maoris to 1840', *The New Zealand Journal of History,* Vol. 2, No. 1, April 1968, pp. 18-40; J. M.

R. Owens, 'Religious Disputation at Whangaroa 1823-7', *JPS*, Vol. 79, No. 3, September 1970, pp. 288-304.

2. Hobbs's Journal, 15 October 1826, TTC. See also Nathaniel Turner-Rev. J. Etchells, 30 September 1824. Compare this with Kendall's investigations into Maori belief, in Binney, pp. 128-31.

3. William White, Letter on Mission Work, 21 September 1824, ATL.

4. Jnl extract, 29 February 1824, in Nathaniel Turner-WMS, 18 June 1824, Uncat. MSS., ML; see also James Stack, Jnl extract, 28 March 1825; Hobbs's Journal, 28 March 1825; Jnl extracts, 1 April, 19 May 1826, in James Stack-WMS, 12 October 1826, Uncat. MSS., ML.

5. Nathaniel Turner-Rev. J. Etchells, 30 September 1824.

6. Hobbs's Journal, 15 October 1826, TTC.

7. Jnl extract, 16 October 1825, in John Hobbs, 21 March 1826.

8. For a description of *taniwha,* see Samuel Leigh, Jnl extracts, 27 April 1823; Jnl extract, 28 September 1825, in John Hobbs, 21 March 1826.

9. Jnl extract, 16 October 1825, in Nathaniel Turner, 20 February 1826. See also Binney, *Legacy of Guilt,* pp. 146-9.

10. Jnl extract, 15 February 1826, in James Stack, 21 March 1826.

11. Nathaniel Turner-Rev. J. Etchells, 30 September 1824.

12. Jnl extract, 16 October 1825, in James Stack, 29 March 1826.

13. James Stack, Jnl extract, 7 February 1825.

14. Jnl extract, 15 September 1823, in Nathaniel Turner-WMS, 28 October 1823, Uncat. MSS., ML.

15. Jnl extract, 19 June 1824, in William White, 24 November 1824.

16. White's Journal, 4, 9 July 1823, TTC; Jnl extract, 21 September 1823, in Nathaniel Turner-WMS, 28 October 1823, Uncat. MSS., ML.

17. Jnl extract, 16 October 1825, in John Hobbs, 21 March 1826; Hobbs's Journal, 31 May 1824, TTC

18. Jnl extract, 5 February 1825, in Nathaniel Turner, 31 March 1825.

19. James Stack, Jnl extract, 9 February 1825.

20. E.g. Samuel Leigh-WMS, 15 November 1823, Uncat. MSS., ML.

21. Jnl extract, 25 January 1825, in Nathaniel Turner-WMS, 31 March 1825.

22. James Stack, Jnl extract, 26 March 1825.

23. Jnl extracts, 1 and 9 October 1825, in James Stack, 29 March 1826.

24. Jnl extract, 6 June 1824, in Nathaniel Turner-WMS, 8 July 1824, Uncat. MSS., ML.

25. Jnl extract, 25 December 1826, in James Stack-WMS, 17 January 1827, Uncat. MSS., ML.

26. Jnl extract, 15 October 1826, in James Stack-WMS, 17 January 1827, Uncat. MSS., ML.
27. Jnl extract, 6 June 1824, in Nathaniel Turner-WMS, 8 July 1824, Uncat. MSS., ML.
28. Hobbs's Journal, 11 July 1824, TTC.
29. Jnl extract, 24 September 1826, in James Stack-WMS, 12 October 1826, Uncat. MSS., ML.
30. Jnl extract, 1 October 1825, in James Stack, 29 March 1826.
31. White's Journal, 7 November 1824, TTC.
32. Hobbs's Journal, 2 July 1825, TTC.
33. Jnl extract, 25 April 1824, in Nathaniel Turner-WMS, 30 June 1824, Uncat. MSS., ML.
34. Jnl extract, 24 September 1826, in John Hobbs, 30 November 1826.
35. Hobbs's Journal, 27 August 1826, TTC.
36. Ibid., 3 October 1824.
37. Jnl extract, 5 March 1826, in James Stack-WMS, 12 October 1826, Uncat. MSS., ML.
38. Jnl extract, 15 October 1825, in James Stack, 29 March 1826.
39. White's Journal, 11 July 1824, TTC.
40. Jnl extract, 15 October 1825, in James Stack, 29 March 1826.
41. Jnl extract, 30 October 1825, in James Stack, 29 March 1826.
42. Hobbs's Journal, 18 July 1824, TTC.
43. Jnl extract, 30 October 1825, in John Hobbs, 22 March 1826.
44. Jnl extract, 4 December 1825, in James Stack, 29 March 1826.
45. Hobbs's Journal, 16 (?) October 1826, TTC.
46. Jnl extract, 9 July 1826, in James Stack-WMS, 12 October 1826, Uncat. MSS., ML.
47. White's Journal, 8 August 1824, TTC; James Stack, Jnl extract, 27 August 1825; Jnl extract, 15 October 1825, in James Stack, 29 March 1826.
48. Jnl extract, 3 November 1825, in James Stack, 29 March 1826.
49. James Stack, Jnl extract, 30 August 1825; Jnl extract, 21 November 1825, in James Stack, 29 March 1826. Much the same question was asked by the North American Indians of John Eliot in the 17th century: S. E. Morison, *Builders of the Bay Colony* (Boston, 1964), pp. 297-8.
50. Stack, op. cit., 21 November 1825.
51. White's Journal, 16 October 1824, TTC. Other references to Maui are in ibid., 3 October 1824; William White, Letter on Mission Work, 21 September 1824, ATL.
52. Jnl extract, 16 November 1825, in James Stack, 29 March 1826.
53. Jnl extract, 9 June 1826, in James Stack-WMS, 12 October 1826, Uncat. MSS., ML.
54. Jnl extract, 26 October 1825, in James Stack, 29 March 1826.
55. James Stack, Jnl extract, 30 August 1825.

56. Jnl extract, 29 October 1826, in James Stack-WMS, 17 January 1827, Uncat. MSS., ML.
57. White's Journal, 1 August 1824, TTC; ibid., 3 October 1824.
58. Jnl extract, 22 May 1826, in James Stack-WMS, 12 October 1826, Uncat. MSS., ML.
59. White's Journal, 22 November 1824, TTC; Jnl extract, 9 June 1826, in James Stack-WMS, 12 October 1826, Uncat. MSS., ML.
60. Jnl extract, 9 June 1826, in John Hobbs, 10 November 1826.
61. William White-Rev. John Butler, 13 July 1823, Rev. J. Butler, Letters and Journals 1819-24, No. 26, HL.
62. Jnl extract, 19 February 1826, in Nathaniel Turner, 22 March 1826.
63. White's Journal, 22 November 1824, TTC.
64. Hobbs's Journal, 31 May 1824, TTC.
65. Jnl extract, 4 March 1825, in Nathaniel Turner-WMS, 31 March 1825, Uncat. MSS., ML.
66. Jnl extract, 22 May 1826, in James Stack-WMS, 12 October 1826, Uncat. MSS., ML.
67. See Binney, p. 128.
68. Hobbs's Journal, 28 March 1825, TTC; James Stack, Jnl extract, 28 March 1825.
69. Jnl extract, 14 November 1825, in James Stack, 29 March 1826.
70. Hobbs's Journal, 28 March 1825, TTC.
71. Jnl extract, 31 August 1823, in Nathaniel Turner-WMS, 27 October 1823, Uncat. MSS., ML.
72. Jnl extract, 19 September 1824, in Nathaniel Turner, 23 November 1824.
73. Jnl extract, 16 July 1826, in James Stack-WMS, 12 October 1826, Uncat. MSS., ML.
74. White's Journal, 19 June 1824, TTC.
75. Nathaniel Turner-Rev. J. Etchells, 30 September 1824.
76. James Stack, Jnl extract, 7 May 1825.
77. Jnl extract, 1 October 1825, in James Stack, 29 March 1826.
78. Jnl extract, 4 December 1825, in Nathaniel Turner, 20 February 1826.
79. Jnl extract, 6 June 1824, in Nathaniel Turner-WMS, 8 July 1824, Uncat. MSS., ML.
80. Hobbs's Journal, 30 March 1825, TTC.
81. Jnl extract, 30 March 1825, in John Hobbs, 10 September 1825.
82. Jnl extract, 28 February 1826, in James Stack-WMS, 12 October 1826, Uncat. MSS., ML; see also James Stack, Jnl extracts, 11 July, 9 August 1825.
83. Jnl extract, 27 August 1826, in James Stack-WMS, 12 October 1826, Uncat. MSS., ML.
84. Hobbs's Journal, 27 November 1823, TTC.
85. Ibid., 18 January 1824.

86. William White, Jnl extract, 12 September 1824.
87. Jnl extract, 9 (?) October 1825, in James Stack, 29 March 1826.
88. Hobbs's Journal, 18 January 1824, TTC.
89. Jnl extract, 20 August 1826, in James Stack-WMS, 12 October 1826, Uncat. MSS., ML; Jnl extract, 16 July 1826, in ibid.
90. Jnl extract, 10 March 1826, in James Stack-WMS, 12 October 1826, Uncat. MSS., ML.
91. Jnl extract, 15 February 1826, in James Stack, 21 March 1826.
92. Jnl extract, 3 December 1826, in James Stack-WMS, 17 January 1827, Uncat. MSS., ML.
93. Hobbs's Journal, 15 February 1824, TTC.
94. White's Journal, 16 October 1824, TTC.
95. Jnl extract, 11 September 1826, in James Stack-WMS, 12 October 1826, Uncat. MSS., ML.
96. White's Journal, 14 March 1824, TTC; Jnl extract, 14 March 1824, in Nathaniel Turner-WMS, 18 June 1824, Uncat. MSS., ML; Hobbs's Journal, 3 April 1825, TTC.
97. Jnl extract, 1 January 1826, in James Stack, 29 March 1826.
98. Jnl extract, 2 March 1826, in James Stack-WMS, 12 October 1826, Uncat. MSS., ML.
99. James Stack, Jnl extract, 5 January 1825.
100. Ibid., 24 January 1825; see also Jnl extract, 23 January 1825, in Nathaniel Turner, 31 March 1825.
101. Edward P. Dozier, 'Differing Reactions to Religious Contacts among North American Indian Societies', *International Congress on America,* 1960, Vol. 34, pp. 161-71. See also A. R. Tippett, *Solomon Islands Christianity. A Study in Growth and Obstruction* (London, 1967), esp. pp. 308-9.
102. Jnl extract, 6 January 1824, in Nathaniel Turner, 30 January 1824.
103. James Stack, Jnl extract, 27 April 1825.
104. Jnl extract, 9 April 1826, in James Stack-WMS, 12 October 1826, Uncat. MSS., ML.
105. The inter-relationship of Maori religion and the Maori sense of kinship is well discussed in J. Prytz Johansen, *The Maori and His Religion in its Non-Ritualistic Aspects* (Copenhagen, 1954). See also his *Studies in Maori Rites and Myths* (Copenhagen, 1958).
106. White's Journal, 3 October 1824, TTC.
107. Jnl extract, 29 October 1826, in John Hobbs, 30 November 1826.
108. Jnl extract, 13 November 1825, in James Stack, 29 March 1826.
109. Jnl extract, 9 November 1825, in Stack, ibid.
110. James Stack, Jnl extract, 19 May 1825.
111. Jnl extract, 6 June 1824, in Nathaniel Turner-WMS, 8 July 1824, Uncat. MSS., ML.

112. James Stack, Jnl extract, 27 February 1825.
113. Jnl extract, 13 May 1826, in James Stack-WMS, 12 October 1826, Uncat. MSS., ML.
114. Jnl extract, 1 October 1825, in James Stack, 29 March 1826.
115. Hobbs's Journal, 22 June 1824, TTC.

LIST OF SOURCES

1. MANUSCRIPT EARLY SOURCES

BONWICK TRANSCRIPTS. Missionary, Vol. 5, Mitchell Library.

BUTLER, J. Letters and Journals, 1819-24, Hocken Library, University of Otago.

CHURCH MISSIONARY SOCIETY. Microfilmed archives of the CMS, London, relating to the Australian and New Zealand missions 1808-84, Reel 67, CH/057, Alexander Turnbull Library.

CLARKE, GEORGE. Letters and Journals, 1822-49, Vol. I, Hocken Library, University of Otago.

FERGUSON, JOHN ALEXANDER. Wesleyan Missionary Society, typescript and manuscript copies of the records of missions, including New Zealand, 1823-7, The Australian National Library.

FERGUSON, JOHN ALEXANDER. Wesleyan Missionary Society Records, 1819-26. (Copies of letters from W. Lawry, N.S.W., S. Leigh, N.Z. and others. Extracts from the minutes of the Sydney Committee for the South Sea Missions, 1823 . . . etc.), 1 vol., The Australian National Library.

'GEORGE'. Open letter dictated by, Wesleydale, Whangaroa, 6 November 1823, The Brisbane Documents, Series 12-17, Box IV, The Australian National Library.

HOBBS, JOHN. Journal, 6 October 1823-December 1840, Trinity Theological College.

HOBBS, JOHN. Wesley Dale, N.Z., 28 June 1824-WMS, Typescript, Alexander Turnbull Library.

KEMP, JAMES. Correspondence of . . . 1823-6, Auckland Public Library.

KENT, JOHN RODOLPHUS. 'Journal of Proceedings of His Majesty's Colonial Cutter Mermaid from the 8th Day of May to the 15th Day of August 1823 inclusive, Kept by John Rodolphus Kent, Commander', Mitchell Library.

KING, JOHN. Letters and Journals, 1819-53, Hocken Library, University of Otago.

LAWRY, WALTER. Diary of . . . 1818-25, Mitchell Library (typescript, Auckland Institute and Museum).

LAWRY, WALTER. Ship St. Michael, N.Z., to his parents in Cornwall, 25 July 1822, Alexander Turnbull Library.

[MARSDEN, SAMUEL]. Marsden Papers, Vol. 3, New Zealand Missions 1816-37, Mitchell Library.

MARSDEN, SAMUEL. Correspondence and Letters, 1819-38, Vol. IV, Hocken Library, University of Otago.

179

METHODIST MISSIONARY SOCIETY ARCHIVES, LONDON.
   Papers concerning property and land.
   Inward Correspondence—
      Australia I, 1812-26.
      Australia II, 1827-36.
      Australia III, 1835-43.
      Friendly Islands, 1822-32.
      Friendly Islands, 1832-5.
      Friendly Islands, 1836-7.
      Friendly Islands, 1838-43.
      Tasmania I, 1823-36.
      Tasmania II, 1837-57.
      New Zealand I, 1819-34.
      New Zealand II, 1835-40.
   (Note: much of the New Zealand material of MMS is available on microfilm at the Alexander Turnbull Library, or in typescript at Trinity Theological College.)

OLD LAND CLAIM. No. 938, National Archives.

ORTON, J. Journal 1840-1, Mitchell Library.

TURNER, NATHANIEL. Personal Narrative of . . ., 2 vols. Mitchell Library.

UNCATALOGUED MSS. Set 197, Item 1, Methodist Church Papers— New Zealand, South Seas, Mitchell Library.

WESLEYAN MISSION PAPERS. No. 1, N.S.W. Letters from WMS, London, 1823-8, MSS. Papers 66, Alexander Turnbull Library.

WESLEYAN MISSIONARY LETTERS, 1823-64. Alexander Turnbull Library.

WHITE, WILLIAM. Journal, 16 May 1823-21 September 1835, Trinity Theological College.

WHITE, WILLIAM. Letter on Mission Work, Wesley Dale, Wangaloa [Whangaroa], New Zealand, 21 September 1824, Alexander Turnbull Library.

[WILLIAMS, HENRY]. New Zealand Mission C N/O Rev. H. Williams (a) Letters 1823-35, Micro. MSS. 222, Alexander Turnbull Library.

WILLIAMS PAPERS. Letters and Journals written by the Reverend Henry and Mrs Marianne Williams and the Reverend William and Mrs Jane Williams, 1822-64, Alexander Turnbull Library (typescript Auckland Public Library).

WILLIAMS, WILLIAM. Journal, 1825-76, Alexander Turnbull Library (typescript Auckland Public Library).

II. PRINTED EARLY SOURCES

BARTON, R. J. (COMP.). *Earliest New Zealand: the journals and correspondence of the Rev. John Butler,* Masterton, 1927.

CHAPMAN, SIR FREDERICK R. (ED.). *Journal kept in New Zealand in 1820 by Ensign Alexander McCrae,* Wellington, 1928.

CRUISE, RICHARD A. *Journal of a ten months' residence in New Zealand (1820),* ed. A. G. Bagnall, Christchurch, 1957.

DILLON, PETER. *Narrative and Successful Result of a Voyage in the South Seas, Performed by Order of the Government of British India, to ascertain the Actual Fate of La Perouse's Expedition, interspersed with Accounts of the Religion, Manners, Customs, and Cannibal Practices of the South Sea Islanders,* 2 vols., London, 1829.

EARLE, AUGUSTUS. *Narrative of a Residence in New Zealand,* ed. E. H. McCormick, Oxford, 1966.

ELDER, J. R. (ED.). *The Letters and Journals of Samuel Marsden, 1765-1838,* Dunedin, 1932.

ELDER, J. R. *Marsden's Lieutenants,* Dunedin, 1934.

McNAB, R. (ED.). *Historical Records of New Zealand,* 2 vols., Wellington, 1908, 1914.

MARKHAM, EDWARD. *New Zealand or Recollections of it,* ed. E. H. McCormick, Wellington, 1963.

MONTGOMERY, JAMES, (ED.). *Journal of voyages and travels, by Daniel Tyerman and George Bennet, deputed from the London Missionary Society to visit their various stations in the South Sea islands, China, India, etc., between the years 1821 and 1829,* London, 1831.

NEW ZEALAND NARRATIVE BY THE WESLEYAN MISSIONARIES. Sydney, R. Howe, Government Printer, Uncat. MSS., Mitchell Library.

NICHOLAS, JOHN LIDDIARD. *Narrative of a Voyage to New Zealand,* 2 vols., London, 1817.

ROGERS, LAWRENCE M. (ED.). *The Early Journals of Henry Williams, Senior Missionary in New Zealand of the Church Missionary Society, 1826-40,* Christchurch, 1961.

WRIGHT, OLIVE (TRANS.). *New Zealand 1826-1827; an English translation of the Voyage de l'Astrolabe in New Zealand waters . . .,* Wellington, 1950.

III. EARLY NEWSPAPERS, PERIODICALS, MISSIONARY JOURNALS

CHURCH MISSIONARY RECORD. November 1833.

CHURCH MISSIONARY REGISTER. 1827.

MISSIONARY NOTICES. May 1822.

MISSIONARY REGISTER. February 1822; August 1822.

NEW ZEALAND HERALD. 26 November 1875.

SYDNEY GAZETTE. 17 July 1808; 31 July 1819; 25 April 1827; 27 August 1827.

IV. EARLY PUBLISHED WORKS

BERRY, ALEXANDER. *Reminiscences of . . .,* Sydney, 1912.

CARLETON, HUGH. *The Life of Henry Williams, Archdeacon of Waimate,* 2 vols., Auckland, 1874, 1877.

IRVING, EDWARD. *The Collected Writings of . . .,* Vol. I, London, 1864.

MOISTER, W. *Missionary Worthies,* London, 1885.

POLACK, JOEL S. *New Zealand: being a narrative of travels and adventures during a residence in that country between the years 1831 and 1837,* 2 vols., London, 1838.

POLACK, JOEL S. *Manners and Customs of the New Zealanders*, 2 vols., London, 1840.

REEVES, WILLIAM PEMBER. *The Long White Cloud*, London, 1898.

SAUNDERS, ALFRED. *History of New Zealand*, Vol. I, Christchurch, 1896.

SHERRIN, R. A. A. AND J. H. WALLACE. *Early History of New Zealand*, Auckland, 1890.

STRACHAN, ALEXANDER. *Remarkable Incidents in the Life of the Rev. Samuel Leigh, missionary to the settlers and savages of Australia and New Zealand, with a succinct history of the origin and progress of the missions in those colonies*, London, 1853.

TAYLOR, RICHARD. *Te Ika A Maui, or New Zealand and its inhabitants . . . together with the geology, natural history, productions, and climate of the country*, London, 1870.

THOMSON, ARTHUR S. *The Story of New Zealand, past and present—savage and civilized*, 2 vols., London, 1859.

TURNER, JOSIAH G. *The Pioneer Missionary: Life of the Rev. Nathaniel Turner, missionary in New Zealand, Tonga and Australia by his son . . .*, London, 1872.

WILLIAMS, WILLIAM. *Christianity Among the New Zealanders*, London, 1867.

V. LATER PUBLISHED WORKS

(a) *Books, Pamphlets*

BINNEY, JUDITH. *The Legacy of Guilt, A Life of Thomas Kendall*, Auckland, 1968.

COWAN, JAMES. *A Trader in Cannibal Land, The Life and Adventures of Captain Tapsell*, Dunedin, 1935.

FINDLAY, G. G. AND W. W. HOLDSWORTH. *The History of the Wesleyan Methodist Missionary Society*, Vol. III, London, 1921.

JOHANSEN, J. PRYTZ. *The Maori and his religion in its non-ritualistic aspects*, Copenhagen, 1954.

JOHANSEN, J. PRYTZ. *Studies in Maori Rites and Myths*, Copenhagen, 1958.

KELLY, LESLIE G. *Marion Dufresne at the Bay of Islands*, Wellington, 1951.

McLINTOCK, A. H. (ED.). *An Encylopaedia of New Zealand*, 3 vols., Wellington, 1966.

McNAB, ROBERT. *From Tasman to Marsden, a history of northern New Zealand from 1642 to 1818*, Dunedin, 1914.

MORISON, S. E. *Builders of the Bay Colony*, Boston, 1964.

SCHOLEFIELD, GUY H. (ED.). *A Dictionary of New Zealand Biography*, 2 vols., Wellington, 1940.

SCHWIMMER, ERIC. *The World of the Maori*, Wellington, 1966.

SELIGMAN, EDWIN R. A. (ED.). *Encyclopaedia of the Social Sciences*, 15 vols., New York, 1930-4.

SHARP, ANDREW. *Crisis at Kerikeri*, Wellington, 1958.

SHAW, A. G. L. AND C. M. CLARK (SECTION EDITORS). *Australian Dictionary of Biography, Vols. I-II, 1788-1850*, Melbourne, 1966, 1967.

Sills, David L. (ed.). *International Encyclopedia of the Social Sciences,* 17 vols., New York, 1968.

Sinclair, Keith. *A History of New Zealand,* Revised edition, Harmondsworth, 1969.

Smith, Stephenson Percy. *Maori Wars of the Nineteenth Century; the struggle of the northern against the southern Maori tribes prior to the colonization of New Zealand in 1840,* Christchurch, 1910.

Thrupp, Sylvia L. (ed.) *Millennial Dreams in Action: essays in comparative study,* Hague, 1962.

Tippett, A. R. *Solomon Islands Christianity, A Study in Growth and Obstruction,* London, 1967.

Wright, Harrison. *New Zealand, 1769-1840: Early Years of Western Contact,* Cambridge, Massachusetts, 1959.

(b) *Periodical articles*

Dozier, Edward P. 'Differing Reactions to Religious Contacts among North American Indian Societies', *International Congress on America,* 1960, Vol. 34, pp. 161-71.

Gluckman, Max. 'The Peace in the Feud', *Past and Present,* 1955, No. 8, pp. 1-14.

Hames, E. W. 'Walter Lawry and the Wesleyan Mission in the South Seas', *Wesley Historical Society (New Zealand) Proceedings,* Vol. 23, No. 4, September 1967.

Kelly, Leslie G. 'Some new information concerning the ship Boyd', *JPS,* Vol. 49, No. 196, December 1940, p. 600.

Linton, Ralph. 'Nativistic Movements', *American Anthropologist,* Vol. 45, 1943, pp. 230-40.

Owens, J. M. R. 'Christianity and the Maoris to 1840', *The New Zealand Journal of History,* Vol. 2, No. 1, April 1968, pp. 18-40.

Owens, J. M. R. 'Religious Disputation at Whangaroa 1823-7', *JPS,* Vol. 79, No. 3, September 1970, pp. 288-304.

Smith, S. Percy. 'The Peopling of the North', *JPS,* Vol. 6, 1897, Supplement.

VI. UNPUBLISHED THESIS

Gunson, W. N. 'Evangelical Missionaries in the South Seas 1797-1860' (Unpublished thesis, Australian National University, 1959).

VII. BIBLIOGRAPHICAL GUIDES

Alington, Margaret H. Letters and other material relative to Australia, New Zealand and the South Seas in the possession of the Methodist Missionary Society, London, March 1957, typescript Alexander Turnbull Library.

Ferguson, John Alexander. Wesleyan Missionary Society Records. Summary of original documents in the Mitchell Library, typescript, Australian National Library.

Hitchings, M. G. Church Missionary Society, London. Guide to the microfilmed archives relating to the Australian and New Zealand Missions, 1959, typescript, Alexander Turnbull Library.

INDEX